C-2233   CAREER EXAMINATION SERIES

This is your
PASSBOOK for...

Advanced Clerical and Secretarial Positions

Test Preparation Study Guide
Questions & Answers

COPYRIGHT NOTICE

This book is SOLELY intended for, is sold ONLY to, and its use is RESTRICTED to individual, bona fide applicants or candidates who qualify by virtue of having seriously filed applications for appropriate license, certificate, professional and/or promotional advancement, higher school matriculation, scholarship, or other legitimate requirements of education and/or governmental authorities.

This book is NOT intended for use, class instruction, tutoring, training, duplication, copying, reprinting, excerption, or adaptation, etc., by:

1) Other publishers
2) Proprietors and/or Instructors of "Coaching" and/or Preparatory Courses
3) Personnel and/or Training Divisions of commercial, industrial, and governmental organizations
4) Schools, colleges, or universities and/or their departments and staffs, including teachers and other personnel
5) Testing Agencies or Bureaus
6) Study groups which seek by the purchase of a single volume to copy and/or duplicate and/or adapt this material for use by the group as a whole without having purchased individual volumes for each of the members of the group
7) Et al.

Such persons would be in violation of appropriate Federal and State statutes.

PROVISION OF LICENSING AGREEMENTS – Recognized educational, commercial, industrial, and governmental institutions and organizations, and others legitimately engaged in educational pursuits, including training, testing, and measurement activities, may address request for a licensing agreement to the copyright owners, who will determine whether, and under what conditions, including fees and charges, the materials in this book may be used them. In other words, a licensing facility exists for the legitimate use of the material in this book on other than an individual basis. However, it is asseverated and affirmed here that the material in this book CANNOT be used without the receipt of the express permission of such a licensing agreement from the Publishers. Inquiries re licensing should be addressed to the company, attention rights and permissions department.

All rights reserved, including the right of reproduction in whole or in part, in any form or by any means, electronic or mechanical, including photocopying, recording, or by any information storage and retrieval system, without permission in writing from the Publisher.

Copyright © 2024 by
National Learning Corporation

212 Michael Drive, Syosset, NY 11791
(516) 921-8888 • www.passbooks.com
E-mail: info@passbooks.com

PUBLISHED IN THE UNITED STATES OF AMERICA

PASSBOOK® SERIES

THE *PASSBOOK® SERIES* has been created to prepare applicants and candidates for the ultimate academic battlefield – the examination room.

At some time in our lives, each and every one of us may be required to take an examination – for validation, matriculation, admission, qualification, registration, certification, or licensure.

Based on the assumption that every applicant or candidate has met the basic formal educational standards, has taken the required number of courses, and read the necessary texts, the *PASSBOOK® SERIES* furnishes the one special preparation which may assure passing with confidence, instead of failing with insecurity. Examination questions – together with answers – are furnished as the basic vehicle for study so that the mysteries of the examination and its compounding difficulties may be eliminated or diminished by a sure method.

This book is meant to help you pass your examination provided that you qualify and are serious in your objective.

The entire field is reviewed through the huge store of content information which is succinctly presented through a provocative and challenging approach – the question-and-answer method.

A climate of success is established by furnishing the correct answers at the end of each test.

You soon learn to recognize types of questions, forms of questions, and patterns of questioning. You may even begin to anticipate expected outcomes.

You perceive that many questions are repeated or adapted so that you can gain acute insights, which may enable you to score many sure points.

You learn how to confront new questions, or types of questions, and to attack them confidently and work out the correct answers.

You note objectives and emphases, and recognize pitfalls and dangers, so that you may make positive educational adjustments.

Moreover, you are kept fully informed in relation to new concepts, methods, practices, and directions in the field.

You discover that you are actually taking the examination all the time: you are preparing for the examination by "taking" an examination, not by reading extraneous and/or supererogatory textbooks.

In short, this PASSBOOK®, used directedly, should be an important factor in helping you to pass your test.

ADVANCED CLERICAL AND SECRETARIAL POSITIONS

STATE GOVERNMENT

1. Clerk 3
2. Clerk Typist 3
3. Executive Secretary 1
4. Secretarial Supervisor 1
5. Secretarial Supervisor 2
6. Clerical Supervisor 1
7. Clerical Supervisor 2

LOCAL GOVERNMENT

8. Clerk 3
9. Clerk Typist 3
10. Executive Secretary
11. Secretarial Supervisor 1
12. Secretarial Supervisor 2
13. Clerical Supervisor 1
14. Clerical Supervisor 2

Clerks 3 perform advanced clerical duties, such as gathering and providing information, sorting, filing and checking materials.

Clerk Typists 3 perform advanced clerical duties, such as typing complex materials, composing letters and memoranda.

Executive Secretaries perform secretarial work as staff assistants to agency executive staff. Supervision may be exercised over a small clerical staff.

Secretarial Supervisors provide secretarial and clerical services to an office and supervise employees who perform moderately complex secretarial and clerical duties.

Clerical Supervisors are working supervisors who supervise employees who perform routine and/or moderately complex clerical duties.

All Clerical and Secretarial Supervisors assign and review work and are responsible for training, employee development and performance evaluation. Work at the 2 level is characterized by the increased complexity, variety and diversity of activities supervised.

Subject Areas	Clerk 3, Clerk Typist 3 Executive Secretary	Secretarial/ Clerical Supervisor 1, 2
Office Procedures and Practices	20	20
Spelling	10	10
Punctuation and Capitalization	10	10
Grammar	10	10
Proofreading	25	25
Arithmetic Computation	10	10
Office Management and Planning	20	20
Data Processing	20	20

Typing Test

You do not need previous computer experience to take the test. There is a 5-minute practice exercise followed by the 5-minute typing test. The passing score is 40 wpm (after deduction for errors). If your score is less than 40 wpm, you will immediately be given a second chance to take and pass the test. You must pass the typing test in order to take the multiple-choice test for Clerk Typist 3 or Executive Secretary.

HOW TO TAKE A TEST

I. YOU MUST PASS AN EXAMINATION

A. *WHAT EVERY CANDIDATE SHOULD KNOW*

Examination applicants often ask us for help in preparing for the written test. What can I study in advance? What kinds of questions will be asked? How will the test be given? How will the papers be graded?

As an applicant for a civil service examination, you may be wondering about some of these things. Our purpose here is to suggest effective methods of advance study and to describe civil service examinations.

Your chances for success on this examination can be increased if you know how to prepare. Those "pre-examination jitters" can be reduced if you know what to expect. You can even experience an adventure in good citizenship if you know why civil service exams are given.

B. *WHY ARE CIVIL SERVICE EXAMINATIONS GIVEN?*

Civil service examinations are important to you in two ways. As a citizen, you want public jobs filled by employees who know how to do their work. As a job seeker, you want a fair chance to compete for that job on an equal footing with other candidates. The best-known means of accomplishing this two-fold goal is the competitive examination.

Exams are widely publicized throughout the nation. They may be administered for jobs in federal, state, city, municipal, town or village governments or agencies.

Any citizen may apply, with some limitations, such as the age or residence of applicants. Your experience and education may be reviewed to see whether you meet the requirements for the particular examination. When these requirements exist, they are reasonable and applied consistently to all applicants. Thus, a competitive examination may cause you some uneasiness now, but it is your privilege and safeguard.

C. *HOW ARE CIVIL SERVICE EXAMS DEVELOPED?*

Examinations are carefully written by trained technicians who are specialists in the field known as "psychological measurement," in consultation with recognized authorities in the field of work that the test will cover. These experts recommend the subject matter areas or skills to be tested; only those knowledges or skills important to your success on the job are included. The most reliable books and source materials available are used as references. Together, the experts and technicians judge the difficulty level of the questions.

Test technicians know how to phrase questions so that the problem is clearly stated. Their ethics do not permit "trick" or "catch" questions. Questions may have been tried out on sample groups, or subjected to statistical analysis, to determine their usefulness.

Written tests are often used in combination with performance tests, ratings of training and experience, and oral interviews. All of these measures combine to form the best-known means of finding the right person for the right job.

II. HOW TO PASS THE WRITTEN TEST

A. NATURE OF THE EXAMINATION

To prepare intelligently for civil service examinations, you should know how they differ from school examinations you have taken. In school you were assigned certain definite pages to read or subjects to cover. The examination questions were quite detailed and usually emphasized memory. Civil service exams, on the other hand, try to discover your present ability to perform the duties of a position, plus your potentiality to learn these duties. In other words, a civil service exam attempts to predict how successful you will be. Questions cover such a broad area that they cannot be as minute and detailed as school exam questions.

In the public service similar kinds of work, or positions, are grouped together in one "class." This process is known as *position-classification*. All the positions in a class are paid according to the salary range for that class. One class title covers all of these positions, and they are all tested by the same examination.

B. FOUR BASIC STEPS

1) Study the announcement

How, then, can you know what subjects to study? Our best answer is: "Learn as much as possible about the class of positions for which you've applied." The exam will test the knowledge, skills and abilities needed to do the work.

Your most valuable source of information about the position you want is the official exam announcement. This announcement lists the training and experience qualifications. Check these standards and apply only if you come reasonably close to meeting them.

The brief description of the position in the examination announcement offers some clues to the subjects which will be tested. Think about the job itself. Review the duties in your mind. Can you perform them, or are there some in which you are rusty? Fill in the blank spots in your preparation.

Many jurisdictions preview the written test in the exam announcement by including a section called "Knowledge and Abilities Required," "Scope of the Examination," or some similar heading. Here you will find out specifically what fields will be tested.

2) Review your own background

Once you learn in general what the position is all about, and what you need to know to do the work, ask yourself which subjects you already know fairly well and which need improvement. You may wonder whether to concentrate on improving your strong areas or on building some background in your fields of weakness. When the announcement has specified "some knowledge" or "considerable knowledge," or has used adjectives like "beginning principles of…" or "advanced … methods," you can get a clue as to the number and difficulty of questions to be asked in any given field. More questions, and hence broader coverage, would be included for those subjects which are more important in the work. Now weigh your strengths and weaknesses against the job requirements and prepare accordingly.

3) Determine the level of the position

Another way to tell how intensively you should prepare is to understand the level of the job for which you are applying. Is it the entering level? In other words, is this the position in which beginners in a field of work are hired? Or is it an intermediate or advanced level? Sometimes this is indicated by such words as "Junior" or "Senior" in the class title. Other jurisdictions use Roman numerals to designate the level – Clerk I, Clerk II, for example. The word "Supervisor" sometimes appears in the title. If the level is not indicated by the title, check the description of duties. Will you be working under very close supervision, or will you have responsibility for independent decisions in this work?

4) Choose appropriate study materials

Now that you know the subjects to be examined and the relative amount of each subject to be covered, you can choose suitable study materials. For beginning level jobs, or even advanced ones, if you have a pronounced weakness in some aspect of your training, read a modern, standard textbook in that field. Be sure it is up to date and has general coverage. Such books are normally available at your library, and the librarian will be glad to help you locate one. For entry-level positions, questions of appropriate difficulty are chosen – neither highly advanced questions, nor those too simple. Such questions require careful thought but not advanced training.

If the position for which you are applying is technical or advanced, you will read more advanced, specialized material. If you are already familiar with the basic principles of your field, elementary textbooks would waste your time. Concentrate on advanced textbooks and technical periodicals. Think through the concepts and review difficult problems in your field.

These are all general sources. You can get more ideas on your own initiative, following these leads. For example, training manuals and publications of the government agency which employs workers in your field can be useful, particularly for technical and professional positions. A letter or visit to the government department involved may result in more specific study suggestions, and certainly will provide you with a more definite idea of the exact nature of the position you are seeking.

III. KINDS OF TESTS

Tests are used for purposes other than measuring knowledge and ability to perform specified duties. For some positions, it is equally important to test ability to make adjustments to new situations or to profit from training. In others, basic mental abilities not dependent on information are essential. Questions which test these things may not appear as pertinent to the duties of the position as those which test for knowledge and information. Yet they are often highly important parts of a fair examination. For very general questions, it is almost impossible to help you direct your study efforts. What we can do is to point out some of the more common of these general abilities needed in public service positions and describe some typical questions.

1) General information

Broad, general information has been found useful for predicting job success in some kinds of work. This is tested in a variety of ways, from vocabulary lists to questions about current events. Basic background in some field of work, such as sociology or economics, may be sampled in a group of questions. Often these are principles which have become familiar to most persons through exposure rather than through formal training. It is difficult to advise you how to study for these questions; being alert to the world around you is our best suggestion.

2) Verbal ability

An example of an ability needed in many positions is verbal or language ability. Verbal ability is, in brief, the ability to use and understand words. Vocabulary and grammar tests are typical measures of this ability. Reading comprehension or paragraph interpretation questions are common in many kinds of civil service tests. You are given a paragraph of written material and asked to find its central meaning.

3) Numerical ability

Number skills can be tested by the familiar arithmetic problem, by checking paired lists of numbers to see which are alike and which are different, or by interpreting charts and graphs. In the latter test, a graph may be printed in the test booklet which you are asked to use as the basis for answering questions.

4) Observation

A popular test for law-enforcement positions is the observation test. A picture is shown to you for several minutes, then taken away. Questions about the picture test your ability to observe both details and larger elements.

5) Following directions

In many positions in the public service, the employee must be able to carry out written instructions dependably and accurately. You may be given a chart with several columns, each column listing a variety of information. The questions require you to carry out directions involving the information given in the chart.

6) Skills and aptitudes

Performance tests effectively measure some manual skills and aptitudes. When the skill is one in which you are trained, such as typing or shorthand, you can practice. These tests are often very much like those given in business school or high school courses. For many of the other skills and aptitudes, however, no short-time preparation can be made. Skills and abilities natural to you or that you have developed throughout your lifetime are being tested.

Many of the general questions just described provide all the data needed to answer the questions and ask you to use your reasoning ability to find the answers. Your best preparation for these tests, as well as for tests of facts and ideas, is to be at your physical and mental best. You, no doubt, have your own methods of getting into an exam-taking mood and keeping "in shape." The next section lists some ideas on this subject.

IV. KINDS OF QUESTIONS

Only rarely is the "essay" question, which you answer in narrative form, used in civil service tests. Civil service tests are usually of the short-answer type. Full instructions for answering these questions will be given to you at the examination. But in case this is your first experience with short-answer questions and separate answer sheets, here is what you need to know:

1) Multiple-choice Questions

Most popular of the short-answer questions is the "multiple choice" or "best answer" question. It can be used, for example, to test for factual knowledge, ability to solve problems or judgment in meeting situations found at work.

A multiple-choice question is normally one of three types—
- It can begin with an incomplete statement followed by several possible endings. You are to find the one ending which *best* completes the statement, although some of the others may not be entirely wrong.
- It can also be a complete statement in the form of a question which is answered by choosing one of the statements listed.

- It can be in the form of a problem – again you select the best answer.

Here is an example of a multiple-choice question with a discussion which should give you some clues as to the method for choosing the right answer:

When an employee has a complaint about his assignment, the action which will *best* help him overcome his difficulty is to
    A. discuss his difficulty with his coworkers
    B. take the problem to the head of the organization
    C. take the problem to the person who gave him the assignment
    D. say nothing to anyone about his complaint

In answering this question, you should study each of the choices to find which is best. Consider choice "A" – Certainly an employee may discuss his complaint with fellow employees, but no change or improvement can result, and the complaint remains unresolved. Choice "B" is a poor choice since the head of the organization probably does not know what assignment you have been given, and taking your problem to him is known as "going over the head" of the supervisor. The supervisor, or person who made the assignment, is the person who can clarify it or correct any injustice. Choice "C" is, therefore, correct. To say nothing, as in choice "D," is unwise. Supervisors have and interest in knowing the problems employees are facing, and the employee is seeking a solution to his problem.

2) True/False Questions

The "true/false" or "right/wrong" form of question is sometimes used. Here a complete statement is given. Your job is to decide whether the statement is right or wrong.

SAMPLE: A roaming cell-phone call to a nearby city costs less than a non-roaming call to a distant city.

This statement is wrong, or false, since roaming calls are more expensive.

This is not a complete list of all possible question forms, although most of the others are variations of these common types. You will always get complete directions for answering questions. Be sure you understand *how* to mark your answers – ask questions until you do.

V. RECORDING YOUR ANSWERS

Computer terminals are used more and more today for many different kinds of exams.

For an examination with very few applicants, you may be told to record your answers in the test booklet itself. Separate answer sheets are much more common. If this separate answer sheet is to be scored by machine – and this is often the case – it is highly important that you mark your answers correctly in order to get credit.

An electronic scoring machine is often used in civil service offices because of the speed with which papers can be scored. Machine-scored answer sheets must be marked with a pencil, which will be given to you. This pencil has a high graphite content which responds to the electronic scoring machine. As a matter of fact, stray dots may register as answers, so do not let your pencil rest on the answer sheet while you are pondering the correct answer. Also, if your pencil lead breaks or is otherwise defective, ask for another.

Since the answer sheet will be dropped in a slot in the scoring machine, be careful not to bend the corners or get the paper crumpled.

The answer sheet normally has five vertical columns of numbers, with 30 numbers to a column. These numbers correspond to the question numbers in your test booklet. After each number, going across the page are four or five pairs of dotted lines. These short dotted lines have small letters or numbers above them. The first two pairs may also have a "T" or "F" above the letters. This indicates that the first two pairs only are to be used if the questions are of the true-false type. If the questions are multiple choice, disregard the "T" and "F" and pay attention only to the small letters or numbers.

Answer your questions in the manner of the sample that follows:

32. The largest city in the United States is
    A. Washington, D.C.
    B. New York City
    C. Chicago
    D. Detroit
    E. San Francisco

1) Choose the answer you think is best. (New York City is the largest, so "B" is correct.)
2) Find the row of dotted lines numbered the same as the question you are answering. (Find row number 32)
3) Find the pair of dotted lines corresponding to the answer. (Find the pair of lines under the mark "B.")
4) Make a solid black mark between the dotted lines.

VI. BEFORE THE TEST

Common sense will help you find procedures to follow to get ready for an examination. Too many of us, however, overlook these sensible measures. Indeed, nervousness and fatigue have been found to be the most serious reasons why applicants fail to do their best on civil service tests. Here is a list of reminders:

- Begin your preparation early – Don't wait until the last minute to go scurrying around for books and materials or to find out what the position is all about.
- Prepare continuously – An hour a night for a week is better than an all-night cram session. This has been definitely established. What is more, a night a week for a month will return better dividends than crowding your study into a shorter period of time.
- Locate the place of the exam – You have been sent a notice telling you when and where to report for the examination. If the location is in a different town or otherwise unfamiliar to you, it would be well to inquire the best route and learn something about the building.
- Relax the night before the test – Allow your mind to rest. Do not study at all that night. Plan some mild recreation or diversion; then go to bed early and get a good night's sleep.
- Get up early enough to make a leisurely trip to the place for the test – This way unforeseen events, traffic snarls, unfamiliar buildings, etc. will not upset you.
- Dress comfortably – A written test is not a fashion show. You will be known by number and not by name, so wear something comfortable.

- Leave excess paraphernalia at home – Shopping bags and odd bundles will get in your way. You need bring only the items mentioned in the official notice you received; usually everything you need is provided. Do not bring reference books to the exam. They will only confuse those last minutes and be taken away from you when in the test room.
- Arrive somewhat ahead of time – If because of transportation schedules you must get there very early, bring a newspaper or magazine to take your mind off yourself while waiting.
- Locate the examination room – When you have found the proper room, you will be directed to the seat or part of the room where you will sit. Sometimes you are given a sheet of instructions to read while you are waiting. Do not fill out any forms until you are told to do so; just read them and be prepared.
- Relax and prepare to listen to the instructions
- If you have any physical problem that may keep you from doing your best, be sure to tell the test administrator. If you are sick or in poor health, you really cannot do your best on the exam. You can come back and take the test some other time.

VII. AT THE TEST

The day of the test is here and you have the test booklet in your hand. The temptation to get going is very strong. Caution! There is more to success than knowing the right answers. You must know how to identify your papers and understand variations in the type of short-answer question used in this particular examination. Follow these suggestions for maximum results from your efforts:

1) Cooperate with the monitor

The test administrator has a duty to create a situation in which you can be as much at ease as possible. He will give instructions, tell you when to begin, check to see that you are marking your answer sheet correctly, and so on. He is not there to guard you, although he will see that your competitors do not take unfair advantage. He wants to help you do your best.

2) Listen to all instructions

Don't jump the gun! Wait until you understand all directions. In most civil service tests you get more time than you need to answer the questions. So don't be in a hurry. Read each word of instructions until you clearly understand the meaning. Study the examples, listen to all announcements and follow directions. Ask questions if you do not understand what to do.

3) Identify your papers

Civil service exams are usually identified by number only. You will be assigned a number; you must not put your name on your test papers. Be sure to copy your number correctly. Since more than one exam may be given, copy your exact examination title.

4) Plan your time

Unless you are told that a test is a "speed" or "rate of work" test, speed itself is usually not important. Time enough to answer all the questions will be provided, but this does not mean that you have all day. An overall time limit has been set. Divide the total time (in minutes) by the number of questions to determine the approximate time you have for each question.

5) Do not linger over difficult questions

If you come across a difficult question, mark it with a paper clip (useful to have along) and come back to it when you have been through the booklet. One caution if you do this – be sure to skip a number on your answer sheet as well. Check often to be sure that you have not lost your place and that you are marking in the row numbered the same as the question you are answering.

6) Read the questions

Be sure you know what the question asks! Many capable people are unsuccessful because they failed to *read* the questions correctly.

7) Answer all questions

Unless you have been instructed that a penalty will be deducted for incorrect answers, it is better to guess than to omit a question.

8) Speed tests

It is often better NOT to guess on speed tests. It has been found that on timed tests people are tempted to spend the last few seconds before time is called in marking answers at random – without even reading them – in the hope of picking up a few extra points. To discourage this practice, the instructions may warn you that your score will be "corrected" for guessing. That is, a penalty will be applied. The incorrect answers will be deducted from the correct ones, or some other penalty formula will be used.

9) Review your answers

If you finish before time is called, go back to the questions you guessed or omitted to give them further thought. Review other answers if you have time.

10) Return your test materials

If you are ready to leave before others have finished or time is called, take ALL your materials to the monitor and leave quietly. Never take any test material with you. The monitor can discover whose papers are not complete, and taking a test booklet may be grounds for disqualification.

VIII. EXAMINATION TECHNIQUES

1) Read the general instructions carefully. These are usually printed on the first page of the exam booklet. As a rule, these instructions refer to the timing of the examination; the fact that you should not start work until the signal and must stop work at a signal, etc. If there are any *special* instructions, such as a choice of questions to be answered, make sure that you note this instruction carefully.

2) When you are ready to start work on the examination, that is as soon as the signal has been given, read the instructions to each question booklet, underline any key words or phrases, such as *least, best, outline, describe* and the like. In this way you will tend to answer as requested rather than discover on reviewing your paper that you *listed without describing*, that you selected the *worst* choice rather than the *best* choice, etc.

3) If the examination is of the objective or multiple-choice type – that is, each question will also give a series of possible answers: A, B, C or D, and you are called upon to select the best answer and write the letter next to that answer on your answer paper – it is advisable to start answering each question in turn. There may be anywhere from 50 to 100 such questions in the three or four hours allotted and you can see how much time would be taken if you read through all the questions before beginning to answer any. Furthermore, if you come across a question or group of questions which you know would be difficult to answer, it would undoubtedly affect your handling of all the other questions.

4) If the examination is of the essay type and contains but a few questions, it is a moot point as to whether you should read all the questions before starting to answer any one. Of course, if you are given a choice – say five out of seven and the like – then it is essential to read all the questions so you can eliminate the two that are most difficult. If, however, you are asked to answer all the questions, there may be danger in trying to answer the easiest one first because you may find that you will spend too much time on it. The best technique is to answer the first question, then proceed to the second, etc.

5) Time your answers. Before the exam begins, write down the time it started, then add the time allowed for the examination and write down the time it must be completed, then divide the time available somewhat as follows:
    - If 3-1/2 hours are allowed, that would be 210 minutes. If you have 80 objective-type questions, that would be an average of 2-1/2 minutes per question. Allow yourself no more than 2 minutes per question, or a total of 160 minutes, which will permit about 50 minutes to review.
    - If for the time allotment of 210 minutes there are 7 essay questions to answer, that would average about 30 minutes a question. Give yourself only 25 minutes per question so that you have about 35 minutes to review.

6) The most important instruction is to *read each question* and make sure you know what is wanted. The second most important instruction is to *time yourself properly* so that you answer every question. The third most important instruction is to *answer every question*. Guess if you have to but include something for each question. Remember that you will receive no credit for a blank and will probably receive some credit if you write something in answer to an essay question. If you guess a letter – say "B" for a multiple-choice question – you may have guessed right. If you leave a blank as an answer to a multiple-choice question, the examiners may respect your feelings but it will not add a point to your score. Some exams may penalize you for wrong answers, so in such cases *only*, you may not want to guess unless you have some basis for your answer.

7) Suggestions
    a. Objective-type questions
        1. Examine the question booklet for proper sequence of pages and questions
        2. Read all instructions carefully
        3. Skip any question which seems too difficult; return to it after all other questions have been answered
        4. Apportion your time properly; do not spend too much time on any single question or group of questions

5. Note and underline key words – *all, most, fewest, least, best, worst, same, opposite,* etc.
6. Pay particular attention to negatives
7. Note unusual option, e.g., unduly long, short, complex, different or similar in content to the body of the question
8. Observe the use of "hedging" words – *probably, may, most likely,* etc.
9. Make sure that your answer is put next to the same number as the question
10. Do not second-guess unless you have good reason to believe the second answer is definitely more correct
11. Cross out original answer if you decide another answer is more accurate; do not erase until you are ready to hand your paper in
12. Answer all questions; guess unless instructed otherwise
13. Leave time for review

b. Essay questions
 1. Read each question carefully
 2. Determine exactly what is wanted. Underline key words or phrases.
 3. Decide on outline or paragraph answer
 4. Include many different points and elements unless asked to develop any one or two points or elements
 5. Show impartiality by giving pros and cons unless directed to select one side only
 6. Make and write down any assumptions you find necessary to answer the questions
 7. Watch your English, grammar, punctuation and choice of words
 8. Time your answers; don't crowd material

8) Answering the essay question

Most essay questions can be answered by framing the specific response around several key words or ideas. Here are a few such key words or ideas:

M's: manpower, materials, methods, money, management
P's: purpose, program, policy, plan, procedure, practice, problems, pitfalls, personnel, public relations
 a. Six basic steps in handling problems:
 1. Preliminary plan and background development
 2. Collect information, data and facts
 3. Analyze and interpret information, data and facts
 4. Analyze and develop solutions as well as make recommendations
 5. Prepare report and sell recommendations
 6. Install recommendations and follow up effectiveness

 b. Pitfalls to avoid
 1. *Taking things for granted* – A statement of the situation does not necessarily imply that each of the elements is necessarily true; for example, a complaint may be invalid and biased so that all that can be taken for granted is that a complaint has been registered

2. *Considering only one side of a situation* – Wherever possible, indicate several alternatives and then point out the reasons you selected the best one
3. *Failing to indicate follow up* – Whenever your answer indicates action on your part, make certain that you will take proper follow-up action to see how successful your recommendations, procedures or actions turn out to be
4. *Taking too long in answering any single question* – Remember to time your answers properly

IX. AFTER THE TEST

Scoring procedures differ in detail among civil service jurisdictions although the general principles are the same. Whether the papers are hand-scored or graded by machine we have described, they are nearly always graded by number. That is, the person who marks the paper knows only the number – never the name – of the applicant. Not until all the papers have been graded will they be matched with names. If other tests, such as training and experience or oral interview ratings have been given, scores will be combined. Different parts of the examination usually have different weights. For example, the written test might count 60 percent of the final grade, and a rating of training and experience 40 percent. In many jurisdictions, veterans will have a certain number of points added to their grades.

After the final grade has been determined, the names are placed in grade order and an eligible list is established. There are various methods for resolving ties between those who get the same final grade – probably the most common is to place first the name of the person whose application was received first. Job offers are made from the eligible list in the order the names appear on it. You will be notified of your grade and your rank as soon as all these computations have been made. This will be done as rapidly as possible.

People who are found to meet the requirements in the announcement are called "eligibles." Their names are put on a list of eligible candidates. An eligible's chances of getting a job depend on how high he stands on this list and how fast agencies are filling jobs from the list.

When a job is to be filled from a list of eligibles, the agency asks for the names of people on the list of eligibles for that job. When the civil service commission receives this request, it sends to the agency the names of the three people highest on this list. Or, if the job to be filled has specialized requirements, the office sends the agency the names of the top three persons who meet these requirements from the general list.

The appointing officer makes a choice from among the three people whose names were sent to him. If the selected person accepts the appointment, the names of the others are put back on the list to be considered for future openings.

That is the rule in hiring from all kinds of eligible lists, whether they are for typist, carpenter, chemist, or something else. For every vacancy, the appointing officer has his choice of any one of the top three eligibles on the list. This explains why the person whose name is on top of the list sometimes does not get an appointment when some of the persons lower on the list do. If the appointing officer chooses the second or third eligible, the No. 1 eligible does not get a job at once, but stays on the list until he is appointed or the list is terminated.

X. HOW TO PASS THE INTERVIEW TEST

The examination for which you applied requires an oral interview test. You have already taken the written test and you are now being called for the interview test – the final part of the formal examination.

You may think that it is not possible to prepare for an interview test and that there are no procedures to follow during an interview. Our purpose is to point out some things you can do in advance that will help you and some good rules to follow and pitfalls to avoid while you are being interviewed.

What is an interview supposed to test?

The written examination is designed to test the technical knowledge and competence of the candidate; the oral is designed to evaluate intangible qualities, not readily measured otherwise, and to establish a list showing the relative fitness of each candidate – as measured against his competitors – for the position sought. Scoring is not on the basis of "right" and "wrong," but on a sliding scale of values ranging from "not passable" to "outstanding." As a matter of fact, it is possible to achieve a relatively low score without a single "incorrect" answer because of evident weakness in the qualities being measured.

Occasionally, an examination may consist entirely of an oral test – either an individual or a group oral. In such cases, information is sought concerning the technical knowledges and abilities of the candidate, since there has been no written examination for this purpose. More commonly, however, an oral test is used to supplement a written examination.

Who conducts interviews?

The composition of oral boards varies among different jurisdictions. In nearly all, a representative of the personnel department serves as chairman. One of the members of the board may be a representative of the department in which the candidate would work. In some cases, "outside experts" are used, and, frequently, a businessman or some other representative of the general public is asked to serve. Labor and management or other special groups may be represented. The aim is to secure the services of experts in the appropriate field.

However the board is composed, it is a good idea (and not at all improper or unethical) to ascertain in advance of the interview who the members are and what groups they represent. When you are introduced to them, you will have some idea of their backgrounds and interests, and at least you will not stutter and stammer over their names.

What should be done before the interview?

While knowledge about the board members is useful and takes some of the surprise element out of the interview, there is other preparation which is more substantive. It *is* possible to prepare for an oral interview – in several ways:

1) Keep a copy of your application and review it carefully before the interview

This may be the only document before the oral board, and the starting point of the interview. Know what education and experience you have listed there, and the sequence and dates of all of it. Sometimes the board will ask you to review the highlights of your experience for them; you should not have to hem and haw doing it.

2) Study the class specification and the examination announcement

Usually, the oral board has one or both of these to guide them. The qualities, characteristics or knowledges required by the position sought are stated in these documents. They offer valuable clues as to the nature of the oral interview. For example, if the job involves supervisory responsibilities, the announcement will usually indicate that knowledge of modern supervisory methods and the qualifications of the candidate as a supervisor will be tested. If so, you can expect such questions, frequently in the form of a hypothetical situation which you are expected to solve. NEVER go into an oral without knowledge of the duties and responsibilities of the job you seek.

3) Think through each qualification required

Try to visualize the kind of questions you would ask if you were a board member. How well could you answer them? Try especially to appraise your own knowledge and background in each area, *measured against the job sought*, and identify any areas in which you are weak. Be critical and realistic – do not flatter yourself.

4) Do some general reading in areas in which you feel you may be weak

For example, if the job involves supervision and your past experience has NOT, some general reading in supervisory methods and practices, particularly in the field of human relations, might be useful. Do NOT study agency procedures or detailed manuals. The oral board will be testing your understanding and capacity, not your memory.

5) Get a good night's sleep and watch your general health and mental attitude

You will want a clear head at the interview. Take care of a cold or any other minor ailment, and of course, no hangovers.

What should be done on the day of the interview?

Now comes the day of the interview itself. Give yourself plenty of time to get there. Plan to arrive somewhat ahead of the scheduled time, particularly if your appointment is in the fore part of the day. If a previous candidate fails to appear, the board might be ready for you a bit early. By early afternoon an oral board is almost invariably behind schedule if there are many candidates, and you may have to wait. Take along a book or magazine to read, or your application to review, but leave any extraneous material in the waiting room when you go in for your interview. In any event, relax and compose yourself.

The matter of dress is important. The board is forming impressions about you – from your experience, your manners, your attitude, and your appearance. Give your personal appearance careful attention. Dress your best, but not your flashiest. Choose conservative, appropriate clothing, and be sure it is immaculate. This is a business interview, and your appearance should indicate that you regard it as such. Besides, being well groomed and properly dressed will help boost your confidence.

Sooner or later, someone will call your name and escort you into the interview room. *This is it.* From here on you are on your own. It is too late for any more preparation. But remember, you asked for this opportunity to prove your fitness, and you are here because your request was granted.

What happens when you go in?

The usual sequence of events will be as follows: The clerk (who is often the board stenographer) will introduce you to the chairman of the oral board, who will introduce you to the other members of the board. Acknowledge the introductions before you sit down. Do not be surprised if you find a microphone facing you or a stenotypist sitting by. Oral interviews are usually recorded in the event of an appeal or other review.

Usually the chairman of the board will open the interview by reviewing the highlights of your education and work experience from your application – primarily for the benefit of the other members of the board, as well as to get the material into the record. Do not interrupt or comment unless there is an error or significant misinterpretation; if that is the case, do not hesitate. But do not quibble about insignificant matters. Also, he will usually ask you some question about your education, experience or your present job – partly to get you to start talking and to establish the interviewing "rapport." He may start the actual questioning, or turn it over to one of the other members. Frequently, each member undertakes the questioning on a particular area, one in which he is perhaps most competent, so you can expect each member to participate in the examination. Because time is limited, you may also expect some rather abrupt switches in the direction the questioning takes, so do not be upset by it. Normally, a board member will not pursue a single line of questioning unless he discovers a particular strength or weakness.

After each member has participated, the chairman will usually ask whether any member has any further questions, then will ask you if you have anything you wish to add. Unless you are expecting this question, it may floor you. Worse, it may start you off on an extended, extemporaneous speech. The board is not usually seeking more information. The question is principally to offer you a last opportunity to present further qualifications or to indicate that you have nothing to add. So, if you feel that a significant qualification or characteristic has been overlooked, it is proper to point it out in a sentence or so. Do not compliment the board on the thoroughness of their examination – they have been sketchy, and you know it. If you wish, merely say, "No thank you, I have nothing further to add." This is a point where you can "talk yourself out" of a good impression or fail to present an important bit of information. Remember, *you close the interview yourself*.

The chairman will then say, "That is all, Mr. _____, thank you." Do not be startled; the interview is over, and quicker than you think. Thank him, gather your belongings and take your leave. Save your sigh of relief for the other side of the door.

How to put your best foot forward

Throughout this entire process, you may feel that the board individually and collectively is trying to pierce your defenses, seek out your hidden weaknesses and embarrass and confuse you. Actually, this is not true. They are obliged to make an appraisal of your qualifications for the job you are seeking, and they want to see you in your best light. Remember, they must interview all candidates and a non-cooperative candidate may become a failure in spite of their best efforts to bring out his qualifications. Here are 15 suggestions that will help you:

1) Be natural – Keep your attitude confident, not cocky

If you are not confident that you can do the job, do not expect the board to be. Do not apologize for your weaknesses, try to bring out your strong points. The board is interested in a positive, not negative, presentation. Cockiness will antagonize any board member and make him wonder if you are covering up a weakness by a false show of strength.

2) Get comfortable, but don't lounge or sprawl

Sit erectly but not stiffly. A careless posture may lead the board to conclude that you are careless in other things, or at least that you are not impressed by the importance of the occasion. Either conclusion is natural, even if incorrect. Do not fuss with your clothing, a pencil or an ashtray. Your hands may occasionally be useful to emphasize a point; do not let them become a point of distraction.

3) Do not wisecrack or make small talk

This is a serious situation, and your attitude should show that you consider it as such. Further, the time of the board is limited – they do not want to waste it, and neither should you.

4) Do not exaggerate your experience or abilities

In the first place, from information in the application or other interviews and sources, the board may know more about you than you think. Secondly, you probably will not get away with it. An experienced board is rather adept at spotting such a situation, so do not take the chance.

5) If you know a board member, do not make a point of it, yet do not hide it

Certainly you are not fooling him, and probably not the other members of the board. Do not try to take advantage of your acquaintanceship – it will probably do you little good.

6) Do not dominate the interview

Let the board do that. They will give you the clues – do not assume that you have to do all the talking. Realize that the board has a number of questions to ask you, and do not try to take up all the interview time by showing off your extensive knowledge of the answer to the first one.

7) Be attentive

You only have 20 minutes or so, and you should keep your attention at its sharpest throughout. When a member is addressing a problem or question to you, give him your undivided attention. Address your reply principally to him, but do not exclude the other board members.

8) Do not interrupt

A board member may be stating a problem for you to analyze. He will ask you a question when the time comes. Let him state the problem, and wait for the question.

9) Make sure you understand the question

Do not try to answer until you are sure what the question is. If it is not clear, restate it in your own words or ask the board member to clarify it for you. However, do not haggle about minor elements.

10) Reply promptly but not hastily

A common entry on oral board rating sheets is "candidate responded readily," or "candidate hesitated in replies." Respond as promptly and quickly as you can, but do not jump to a hasty, ill-considered answer.

11) Do not be peremptory in your answers

A brief answer is proper – but do not fire your answer back. That is a losing game from your point of view. The board member can probably ask questions much faster than you can answer them.

12) Do not try to create the answer you think the board member wants

He is interested in what kind of mind you have and how it works – not in playing games. Furthermore, he can usually spot this practice and will actually grade you down on it.

13) Do not switch sides in your reply merely to agree with a board member

Frequently, a member will take a contrary position merely to draw you out and to see if you are willing and able to defend your point of view. Do not start a debate, yet do not surrender a good position. If a position is worth taking, it is worth defending.

14) Do not be afraid to admit an error in judgment if you are shown to be wrong

The board knows that you are forced to reply without any opportunity for careful consideration. Your answer may be demonstrably wrong. If so, admit it and get on with the interview.

15) Do not dwell at length on your present job

The opening question may relate to your present assignment. Answer the question but do not go into an extended discussion. You are being examined for a *new* job, not your present one. As a matter of fact, try to phrase ALL your answers in terms of the job for which you are being examined.

Basis of Rating

Probably you will forget most of these "do's" and "don'ts" when you walk into the oral interview room. Even remembering them all will not ensure you a passing grade. Perhaps you did not have the qualifications in the first place. But remembering them will help you to put your best foot forward, without treading on the toes of the board members.

Rumor and popular opinion to the contrary notwithstanding, an oral board wants you to make the best appearance possible. They know you are under pressure – but they also want to see how you respond to it as a guide to what your reaction would be under the pressures of the job you seek. They will be influenced by the degree of poise you display, the personal traits you show and the manner in which you respond.

ABOUT THIS BOOK

This book contains tests divided into Examination Sections. Go through each test, answering every question in the margin. We have also attached a sample answer sheet at the back of the book that can be removed and used. At the end of each test look at the answer key and check your answers. On the ones you got wrong, look at the right answer choice and learn. Do not fill in the answers first. Do not memorize the questions and answers, but understand the answer and principles involved. On your test, the questions will likely be different from the samples. Questions are changed and new ones added. If you understand these past questions you should have success with any changes that arise. Tests may consist of several types of questions. We have additional books on each subject should more study be advisable or necessary for you. Finally, the more you study, the better prepared you will be. This book is intended to be the last thing you study before you walk into the examination room. Prior study of relevant texts is also recommended. NLC publishes some of these in our Fundamental Series. Knowledge and good sense are important factors in passing your exam. Good luck also helps. So now study this Passbook, absorb the material contained within and take that knowledge into the examination. Then do your best to pass that exam.

EXAMINATION SECTION

EXAMINATION SECTION
TEST 1

DIRECTIONS: Each question or incomplete statement is followed by several suggested answers or completions. Select the one that BEST answers the question or completes the statement. *PRINT THE LETTER OF THE CORRECT ANSWER IN THE SPACE AT THE RIGHT.*

1. As the supervisor of a staff of clerical employees performing various types of work, you are responsible for the accuracy and efficiency with which their work is performed.
   Of the following actions you may take to insure the accuracy of their work, the MOST practical one is for you to

   A. review each operation completed by a staff member before permitting the employee to proceed to the next operation
   B. keep a record of every error made by an employee and use this record to determine whether a careless employee should be transferred or discharged
   C. assign work in such a way that every operation is performed independently by two employees
   D. determine what errors are likely to occur and set up safeguards to prevent the occurrence of these errors

   1.____

2. Assume that you are the supervisor of a small clerical unit. One of your subordinates has violated a staff regulation by failing to inform you that he will be absent on a certain day.
   Of the following, the MOST appropriate action for you to take first is to

   A. discuss this matter with your immediate superior
   B. find out the reason for his failure to obey this staff regulation
   C. determine what disciplinary action other supervisors have taken in similar cases
   D. take no action if his absence did not interfere with the work of the unit; reprimand him if it did

   2.____

3. A newly appointed clerk is assigned to a unit of an agency at a time when the supervisor of the unit is very busy and has little time to devote to instructing the new employee in the work he is to perform.
   Of the following, the MOST appropriate method of training this employee is for the supervisor to

   A. instruct the new employee to observe several experienced clerks at work and question them regarding any aspect of the work he does not understand
   B. delegate the job of training this employee to an employee in the unit who is qualified to instruct him
   C. assign the new employee a simple task and inform him that more complex and varied duties will be given him when the supervisor is less busy
   D. have the employee spend his time reading the agency's annual reports and the laws, rules, and regulations governing its work

   3.____

4. As a supervisor, you may find it necessary to consult with your superior before taking action on some matters.
   Of the following, the action for which it is MOST important that you obtain the prior approval of your superior is one that involves

   4.____

A. assuming additional functions for your unit
B. rotating assignments among your staff members
C. initiating regular meetings of your staff
D. assigning certain members of your staff to work overtime on an emergency job

5. Suppose that a clerk who is employed in a unit under your supervision performs his work quickly but carelessly. He is about to be transferred to another unit in your department. The chief of this other unit asks you for your opinion of this employee's work habits.
Of the following, the MOST appropriate reply for you to make is to

   A. point out this employee's good qualities only since he may correct his bad qualities after his transfer is effected
   B. say nothing good or bad about this employee, thus permitting him to start his new assignment with a clean slate
   C. inform the unit chief that this clerk performed his work speedily but was careless
   D. emphasize this employee's good points and minimize his bad points

6. When subordinates request his advice in solving problems encountered in their work, a certain bureau chief occasionally answers the request by first asking the subordinate what he thinks should be done.
This action by the bureau chief is, on the whole,

   A. *desirable* because it stimulates subordinates to give more thought to the solution of problems encountered
   B. *undesirable* because it discourages subordinates from asking questions
   C. *desirable* because it discourages subordinates from asking questions
   D. *undesirable* because it undermines the confidence of subordinates in the ability of their supervisor

7. Of the following factors that may be considered by a unit head in dealing with the tardy subordinate, the one which should be given LEAST consideration is the

   A. frequency with which the employee is tardy
   B. effect of the employee's tardiness upon the work of other employees
   C. willingness of the employee to work overtime when necessary
   D. cause of the employee's tardiness

8. Of the following, the action that is likely to contribute MOST to the prestige of a supervisor is for him to

   A. expect all his subordinates to perform with equal efficiency any tasks assigned to them
   B. observe the same rules of conduct that he expects his subordinates to observe
   C. seek their advice on his personal problems and offer them his advice on their personal problems
   D. be always frank and outspoken to his subordinates in pointing out their faults

9. Although an employee under your supervision frequently protests when receiving a monotonous assignment, he nevertheless performs the assigned task efficiently. His protests, however, disturb the other employees and interfere with their work.
Of the following actions you may take in handling this employee, the MOST desirable one is for you to

A. point out to him the effect of his conduct on the staff's work and request his cooperation in accepting such assignments
B. arrange to issue such assignments to him when the other members of his staff are not present
C. inform him that you will request his transfer to another unit unless he puts a halt to his unjustifiable protests
D. ask other members of the staff to tell him that he is disturbing them by his protests

10. Assume that you are the supervisor of a small clerical unit which tabulates data prepared by another unit. One of your employees calls your attention to what appears to be an erroneous figure.
Of the following, the MOST acceptable advice for you to give this employee is to tell him to

10.____

A. omit the figure containing the apparent error and continue with the tabulation
B. make whatever change in the erroneous figure that appears warranted and notify the supervisor of the unit which prepared the data that errors are being made by his staff
C. accept the questionable figure as correct and continue with the tabulation since there is no certainty that an error has been made
D. ask the supervisor of the unit that prepared the data to have the questionable figure checked for accuracy and corrected if it is erroneous

11. A clerk in an agency informs Mr. Brown, an applicant for a license issued by the agency, that the application filed by him was denied because he lacks a year and six months of required experience. Shortly after the applicant leaves the agency's office, the clerk realizes that Mr. Brown lacks only six months of required experience rather than a year and six months.
Of the following, the MOST desirable procedure to be followed in connection with this matter is that

11.____

A. a printed copy of the requirements should be sent to Mr. Brown
B. a letter explaining and correcting the error should be sent to Mr. Brown
C. no action should be taken because Mr. Brown is not qualified at the present time for the license
D. a report of this matter should be prepared and attached to Mr. Brown's application for reference if Mr. Brown should file another application

12. Mr. Stone, who has been recently placed in charge of a clerical unit staffed with ten employees, plans to institute several radical changes in the procedures of his unit.
Of the following actions he may take before adopting any of the revisions, the MOST desirable one is for Mr. Stone to

12.____

A. distribute to each staff member a memorandum describing the revised procedures and requesting the staff's cooperation in giving the revised procedures a fair trial
B. issue to each staff member a memorandum describing the proposed changes and inviting him to submit his written criticism of these proposed changes
C. issue to each staff member a memorandum describing the proposed changes and notifying him of the time and date of a staff conference to be held on the merits of the proposed changes
D. discuss the proposed changes with each staff member independently and obtain his opinion of the proposed changes

13. An assignment completed by Frank King is returned to him by his unit supervisor for certain changes. Frank King objects to making these changes.
    Of the following, the MOST appropriate action for the unit supervisor to take first is to

    A. permit Frank King to present his arguments against making these changes
    B. inform Frank King that he is free to take the matter up with a higher authority
    C. reprimand Frank King for objecting and assign another employee to make these changes
    D. state briefly that his decision is final and indicate by his manner that further discussion would be useless

14. A properly conducted job analysis will reveal the qualities essential for efficient job performance.
    Of the following, the MOST accurate implication of this statement is that job analysis

    A. enables the supervisor to standardize procedures
    B. aids the supervisor in fitting the man to the job
    C. is helpful to the supervisor in scheduling work
    D. assists the supervisor in estimating costs of jobs

15. All of us who are employed by a government agency are, figuratively speaking, living in glass houses.
    Of the following, this quotation MOST nearly means that employees of government agencies are

    A. basically secure in their positions
    B. more closely supervised than are those in private industry
    C. not free to exercise initiative
    D. subject to constant surveillance

16. So important to good supervision is effective leadership that some supervisors who are well equipped in this respect have compensated for deficiencies in other supervisory qualities.
    On the basis of this statement, the MOST accurate of the following statements is that

    A. supervisory ability is the most valuable attribute a leader can have
    B. effective leaders are generally deficient in other supervisory qualities
    C. other supervisory qualities may be substituted for leadership ability
    D. good leaders may make good supervisors even though lacking in other supervisory qualities

17. The improvement in skill and the development of proper attitudes are essential factors in the building of correct work habits.
    Of the following, the MOST valid implication of this statement for a supervisor is that

    A. the more skilled an employee is, the better will be his attitude toward his work
    B. developing proper attitudes in subordinates toward their work is more time-consuming for the supervisor than improving their skill
    C. the improvement of a worker's skill is only part of a supervisor's job
    D. correct work habits are established in order to either improve the skill of workers or develop in them a proper attitude toward their work

Questions 18-21.

DIRECTIONS: Questions 18 through 21 are based upon the situation described below. Consider the facts given in this situation when answering these questions.

SITUATION: *You are the supervisor of a small unit in a large department. In order to assist your staff in handling a peak work load, ten temporary clerks have been hired for a period of two months.*

18. Of the following actions you may take before assigning specific tasks to these temporary employees, the MOST appropriate action is for you to

    A. designate one of their number as your supervisory assistant
    B. find out what clerical experience and training each one has had
    C. ask each member of this group to indicate the type of work he prefers to do
    D. escort this group throughout the department, introducing each temporary employee to all the unit heads in the department

18.____

19. The ten temporary employees have been grouped into two teams of five employees each, and the two teams have been given different assignments. After working with his group for several days, an employee in one group asks to be transferred to the other group.
Of the following reasons for transferring this employee to the other group, the LEAST acceptable one is that

    A. there is a clash in temperament between him and some of the other members of his group
    B. he can perform the work assigned to the other group more efficiently than he can perform the work assigned to his group
    C. the work assigned to the other group is less monotonous than that assigned to his group
    D. the work assigned to his present group compels him to take frequent rest periods because of a physical disability

19.____

20. One of the temporary employees informs you that he has a suggestion for improving the method of performing the work assigned to his group.
Of the following actions, the MOST desirable one for you to take is to

    A. ignore his suggestion since he knows little about the purpose of the assignment
    B. ask him to try out the suggestion before submitting it to you
    C. have him discuss it with his co-workers before submitting it to you
    D. listen to his suggestion and take appropriate action

20.____

21. A temporary clerk who had been decreasing the amount of work he performed and who had also been attempting to induce other temporary clerks to reduce their production was twice cautioned by you to cease these practices. On each occasion, he promised to discontinue these improper practices and to perform his work conscientiously and cooperatively. Soon thereafter, he is detected for the third time attempting to persuade the other temporary clerks to shirk their duties.
Of the following, the MOST appropriate action for you to take is to

21.____

A. reprimand him for his improper conduct and have him transferred immediately to another unit
B. remind him that he may not be employed again as a temporary clerk if he continues his unethical practices
C. call a meeting of the temporary staff and warn them that anyone whose production falls below average will be discharged
D. report his improper practices to your immediate superior and recommend that this employee's services be terminated

22. As a supervisor in an agency, you receive a letter from the head of a civic organization requesting information which you are not permitted to divulge.
In preparing your letter of reply, it is MOST desirable that you

    A. begin with a pleasant phrase or statement and conclude with a brief statement denying the request
    B. limit your reply to a brief statement denying the request
    C. place the denial of the request between a pleasant opening phrase or statement and a cordial closing statement
    D. begin with a denial of the request and conclude with a pleasant closing statement

23. Of the following, it is LEAST essential for a supervisor, in assigning work to a subordinate, to issue written instructions when the

    A. supervisor will be on hand to check the work
    B. instructions are to be passed on to other employees
    C. assignment involves many details
    D. subordinate is to be held strictly accountable for the work performed

24. The suggestion is made that all the secretaries assigned to the bureau chiefs of a certain agency can be transferred to a newly established central transcribing unit which is to be staffed with stenographers and typists. Of the following, the MOST probable effect of reassigning these secretaries would be that

    A. the quality of the stenographic and typing work performed by the secretaries would deteriorate
    B. the bureau chiefs would be burdened with much of the routine work that is now performed by their secretaries
    C. typing and stenographic work would be performed less expeditiously and with frequent delays
    D. the development of understudies for bureau chiefs would be greatly hampered

25. In a large agency where both men and women are employed as clerks, certain duties may be assigned more appropriately to women than to men.
Of the following, the assignment that is generally MOST appropriate for a woman clerk is

    A. sorting and filing 3x5 index cards
    B. issuing supplies from the agency's stockroom to employees presenting requisitions
    C. serving at an information desk during the hours from 7:00 P.M. to 11:00 P.M. for a period of two months
    D. collecting outgoing mail from the various offices of the agency and delivering incoming mail to these offices

26. A unit supervisor discovers several errors in the work performed by a subordinate.
In dealing with this subordinate, it is LEAST desirable for the supervisor to

   A. give his criticism immediately rather than at a later date
   B. make it clear to the subordinate that he is criticizing the subordinate and not the subordinate's work
   C. praise, when possible, some commendable aspect of the subordinate's work before making the adverse criticism
   D. make sure that his criticism is not overheard by other employees

27. The status of the morale of a staff is usually a good indication of the quality of the leadership displayed by the supervisor of the staff.
Of the following, the BEST indication of the existence of high morale among a staff is that

   A. the employees are prompt in reporting for work
   B. the staff is always willing to subordinate personal desires to attain group objectives
   C. it is seldom necessary for the staff to work overtime
   D. the subordinates and their superior meet socially after working hours

28. The use of standard practices and procedures in large organizations is often essential in order to insure a smooth, efficient, and controlled flow of work. A strict adherence to standard practices and procedures to the extent that unnecessary delay is created is known, in general, as *red tape*.
On the basis of this statement, the MOST accurate of the following statements is that

   A. although the use of standard practices and procedures promotes efficiency, it also creates unnecessary delays and *red tape*
   B. in order to insure a smooth, efficient, and controlled plan of work, *red tape* should be eliminated by a strict adherence to standard practices and procedures
   C. *red tape* is a necessary evil which invariably creeps into any large organization which uses standard practices and procedures
   D. *red tape* exists when delay takes place as a result of a too rigid conformity with standard practices and procedures

29. The tasks of government are imposed not only by law but also by public opinion, which at any time may be made into law. Government agencies must, therefore, strive to anticipate and fulfill the needs of the public.
Of the following, the MOST valid implication of this statement is that the

   A. satisfaction of the needs of the public is one of the obligations of a government agency
   B. law prescribes what tasks government agencies should perform and public opinion determines how these tasks should be performed
   C. tasks imposed by law on a government agency have priority over those imposed by public opinion
   D. functions of a government agency should be carried out in accordance with the letter, rather than the spirit, of the law

30. The manner in which an employee performs on the job rather than his potential ability is the true test of his value to his employer.
The one of the following which is NOT an implication of the above statement is a(n)

A. employee of great potential ability may be of little or no value to his employer
B. supervisor should observe the manner in which his subordinates perform their work
C. employee's potential ability is of no significance in determining his fitness for a specific job
D. employee should attempt to perform his work to the best of his ability

31. No routine will automatically bring itself into proper relation with changing conditions. Of the following situations, the one which MOST NEARLY exemplifies the truth of this statement is a

    A. change in the rules governing the submission or reports by employees working in the field is found to be impractical and the previous procedure is reinstituted
    B. long established method of filing papers in a bureau is found to be inadequate because of changes in the functions of the bureau
    C. long established method of distributing orders to the staff is found to work effectively when the size of the staff is considerably increased
    D. change in the rules governing hours of attendance at work proves distasteful to many employees

32. Interest is essentially an attitude of continuing attentiveness, found where activity is satisfactorily self-expressive. Whenever work is so circumscribed that the chance for self-expression or development is denied, monotony is present.
On the basis of this statement, it is MOST accurate to state that

    A. tasks which are repetitive in nature do not permit self-expression and, therefore, create monotony
    B. interest in one's work is increased by financial and non-financial incentives
    C. jobs which are monotonous can be made self-expressive by substituting satisfactory working conditions
    D. workers whose tasks afford them no opportunity for self-expression find such tasks to be monotonous

33. The first step in an organizational study is the reading of the basic documents. There is some documentary basis for any governmental organization, outlining the purposes for which it was established, conferring certain powers, and imposing certain limitations on the conferred powers. This statement indicates that in making an organization study, one should FIRST

    A. review all the authoritative material in the field of government administration and organization
    B. arrange the functions of the organization on a functional chart in accordance with the official documents
    C. study the laws and authorities under which the organization operates
    D. outline the purposes for which the organization study was originally established

34. His attitude is as provincial as an isolationist country's unwillingness to engage in any international trade whatever, on the ground that it will be required to buy something from outsiders which could possibly be produced by local talent, although not as well and not as cheaply. This statement is MOST descriptive of the attitude of the division chief in a government agency who

A. wishes to restrict promotions to supervisory positions in his division exclusively to employees in his division
B. refuses to delegate responsible tasks to subordinates qualified to perform these tasks
C. believes that informal on-the-job training of new staff members is superior to formal training methods
D. frequently makes personal issues out of matters that should be handled on an impersonal basis

35. A trainee was paid a weekly wage of $480.00 for a 40-hour work week. As a result of a new labor contract, he is paid $494.00 a week for a 38-hour work week with time-and-one-half pay for time worked in excess of 38 hours in any work week.
If he continues to work 40 hours weekly under the new contract, the amount by which his average hourly rate for a 40-hour work week under the new contract exceeds the hourly rate previously paid him lies between _____ and _____, inclusive.

    A. $1.02; $1.06   B. $1.08; $1.16   C. $1.18; $1.26   D. $1.28; $1.36

36. The problem of inadequate storage space arising from the large number of inactive records stored in city agencies can be solved MOST satisfactorily with the aid of _____ equipment.

    A. photostat   B. microfilm
    C. IBM sorting   D. digital printing

37. To say that an employee is *erudite* means MOST NEARLY that he is

    A. scholarly
    B. insecure
    C. efficient
    D. punctual

38. The forms design section of a city agency recommended that the sizes of forms used by the agency be limited to the sizes that can be cut with the least amount of waste from either 17" x 22" or 17" x 28" sheets.
Of the following, the size that does NOT comply with this recommendation is

    A. 4 1/2" x 5 1/2"   B. 3 3/4" x 4 1/4"
    C. 3 1/2" x 4 1/4"   D. 4 1/4" x 2 3/4"

39. The number of investigations conducted by an agency in 2007 was 3,600. In 2008, the number of investigations conducted was one-third more than in 2007. The number of investigations conducted in 2009 was three-fourths of the number conducted in 2008. It is anticipated that the number of investigations conducted in 2010 will be equal to the average of the three preceding years.
On the basis of this information, the MOST accurate of the following statements is that the number of investigations conducted in

    A. 2007 is larger than the number anticipated for 2010
    B. 2008 is smaller than the number anticipated for 2010
    C. 2009 is equal to the number conducted in 2007
    D. 2009 is larger than the number anticipated for 2010

40. *The office manager thought it advisable to MOLLIFY his subordinate.*
    The word *mollify* as used in this sentence means MOST NEARLY

    A. reprimand   B. caution   C. calm   D. question

41. *The bureau chief adopted a DILATORY policy.* The word *dilatory* as used in this sentence means MOST NEARLY

    A. tending to cause delay   B. acceptable to all affected
    C. severe but fair   D. prepared with great care

42. *He complained about the PAUCITY of requests.* The word *paucity* as used in this sentence means MOST NEARLY

    A. great variety   B. unreasonableness
    C. unexpected increase   D. scarcity

43. To say that an event is *imminent* means MOST NEARLY that it is

    A. near at hand   B. unpredictable
    C. favorable or happy   D. very significant

44. *The general manager delivered a LAUDATORY speech.*
    The word *laudatory* as used in this sentence means MOST NEARLY

    A. clear and emphatic   B. lengthy
    C. introductory   D. expressing praise

45. *We all knew of his AVERSION for performing statistical work.*
    The word *aversion* as used in this sentence means MOST NEARLY

    A. training   B. dislike
    C. incentive   D. lack of preparation

46. *The engineer was CIRCUMSPECT in making his recommendations.* The word *circumspect* as used in this sentence means MOST NEARLY

    A. hostile   B. outspoken   C. biased   D. cautious

47. To say that certain clerical operations were *obviated* means MOST NEARLY that these operations were

    A. extremely distasteful   B. easily understood
    C. made unnecessary   D. very complicated

48. *The interviewer was impressed with the client's DEMEANOR.* The word *demeanor* as used in this sentence means MOST NEARLY

    A. outward manner   B. plan of action
    C. fluent speech   D. extensive knowledge

49. To say that the information was *gratuitous* means MOST NEARLY that it was

    A. given freely   B. deeply appreciated
    C. brief   D. valuable

50. *The supervisor was unaware of this EXIGENCY.*
    The word *exigency* as used in this sentence means MOST NEARLY

    A. unexplained absence   B. costly delay
    C. pressing need   D. final action

51. *She considered the supervisor's action to be ARBITRARY.* The word *arbitrary* as used in this sentence means MOST NEARLY   51._____

   A. inconsistent
   B. justifiable
   C. appeasing
   D. dictatorial

52. *His report on the activities of the agency was VERBOSE.*   52._____
    The word *verbose* as used in this sentence means MOST NEARLY

   A. vivid   B. wordy   C. vague   D. oral

Questions 53-61.

DIRECTIONS: Questions 53 through 61 are to be answered SOLELY on the basis of the following information.

Assume that the following rules for computing service ratings are to be used experimentally in determining the service ratings of seven permanent employees. (Note that these rules are hypothetical and are NOT to be confused with the existing method of computing service ratings for employees.) The personnel record of each of these seven employees is given in Table II. You are to determine the answer to each of the questions on the basis of the rules given below for computing service ratings and the data contained in the personnel records of these seven employees.

All computations should be made as of the close of the rating period ending March 31, 2007.

RULES FOR COMPUTING SERVICE RATINGS

Service Rating
The service rating of each permanent competitive class employee shall be computed by adding the following three scores: (1) a basic score, (2) the employee's seniority score, and (3) the employee's efficiency score.

Seniority Score
An employee's seniority score shall be computed by crediting him with 1/2% per year for each year of service starting with the date of the employee's entrance as a permanent employee into the competitive class, up to a maximum of 15 years (7 1/2%). A residual fractional period of eight months or more shall be considered as a full year and credited with 1/2%. A residual fraction of from four to, but not including, eight months shall be considered as a half-year and credited with 1/4%. A residual fraction of less than four months shall receive no credit in the seniority score. For example, a person who entered the competitive class as a permanent employee on August 1, 1999 would, as of March 31, 2002, be credited with a seniority score of 1 1/2% for his two years and 8 months of service.

Efficiency Score
An employee's efficiency score shall be computed by adding the annual efficiency ratings received by him during his service in his PRESENT position. (Where there are negative efficiency ratings, such ratings shall be subtracted from the sum of the positive efficiency ratings.) An employee's annual efficiency rating shall be based on the grade he receives from his supervisor for his work performance during the annual efficiency rating period.

Basic Score

A basic score of 70% shall be given to each employee upon permanent appointment to a competitive class position.

An employee shall receive a grade of "A" for performing work of the highest quality and shall be credited with an efficiency rating of plus (+) 3%, An employee shall receive a grade of "F" for performing work of the lowest quality and shall receive an efficiency rating of minus (-) 2%. Table I, entitled "Basis for Determining Annual Efficiency Ratings," lists the six grades of work performance with their equivalent annual efficiency ratings. Table I also lists the efficiency ratings to be assigned for service in a position for less than a year during the annual efficiency rating period. The annual efficiency rating period shall run from April 1 to March 31, inclusive.

TABLE I
BASIS FOE DETERMINING ANNUAL EFFICIENCY RATINGS

Quality of Work Performed	Grade Assigned A	Annual Efficiency Rating for Service in a Position for:		
		8 months to a full year	At least 4 months but less than 8 months	Less than 4 months
Highest Quality	A	+ 3%	+1½%	0%
Good Quality	B	+ 2%	+ 1%	0%
Standard Quality	C	+ 1%	+½%	0%
Substandard Quality	D	0%	0%	0%
Poor Quality	E	-1%	-½%	0%
Lowest Quality	F	-2%	-1%	0%

Appointment or Promotion during an Efficiency Rating Period

An employee who has been appointed or promoted during an efficiency rating period shall receive for that period an efficiency rating only for work performed by him during the portion of the period that he served in the position to which he was appointed or promoted. His efficiency rating for the period shall be determined in accordance with Table I.

Sample Computation of Service Rating

John Smith entered the competitive class as a permanent employee on December 1, 2002 and was promoted to his present position as a Clerk, Grade 3 on November 1, 2005. As a Clerk, Grade 3, he received a grade of "B" for work performed during the five-month period extending from November 1, 2005 to March 31, 2006 and a grade of "C" for work performed during the full annual period extending from April 1, 2006 to March 32, 2007.

On the basis of the Rules for Computing Service Ratings, John Smith should be credited with:

70 % basic score
2 1/4% seniority score - for 4 years and 4 months of service (from 12-1-02 to 3-31-07)
2 % efficiency score - for 5 months of "B" service and a full year of "C" service
74 1/4%

TABLE II
PERSONNEL RECORD OF SEVEN PERMANENT COMPETITIVE CLASS EMPLOYEES

Employee	Present Position	Date of Appointment or Promotion to Present Position	Date of Entry as Permanent Employee in Competitive Class
Allen	Clerk, Gr. 5	6-1-03	7-1-90
Brown	Clerk, Gr. 4	1-1-05	7-1-97
Cole	Clerk, Gr. 3	9-1-03	11-1-00
Fox	Clerk, Gr. 3	10-1-03	9-1-98
Green	Clerk, Gr. 2	12-1-01	12-1-01
Hunt	Clerk, Gr. 2	7-1-02	7-1-02
Kane	Steno, Gr. 3	11-16-04	3-1-01

	Grades Received Annually for Work Performed in Present Position					
Employee	4-1-01 to 3-31-02	4-1-02 to 3-31-03	4-1-03 to 3-31-04	4-1-04 to 3-31-05	4-1-05 to 3-31-06	4-1-06 to 3-31-07
Allen			C*	C	B	C
Brown				C*	C	B
Cole			A*	B	C	C
Fox			C*	C	D	C
Green	C*	D	C	D	C	C
Hunt		C*	C	E	C	C
Kane				B*	B	C

Explanatory Notes:

* Served in present position for less than a full year during this rating period. (Note date of appointment, or promotion, to present period.)

All seven employees have served continuously as permanent employees since their entry into the competitive class.

Questions 53 through 61 refer to the employees listed in Table II. You are to answer these questions SOLELY on the basis of the preceding Rules for Computing Service Ratings and on the information concerning these seven employees given in Table II. You are reminded that all computations are to be made as of the close of the rating period ending March 31, 2007. Candidates may find it helpful to arrange their computations on their scratch paper in an orderly manner since the computations for one question may also be utilized in answering another question.

53. The seniority score of Allen is
    A. 74%   B. 8 1/2%   C. 8%   D. 8 1/4%

54. The seniority score of Fox exceeds that of Cole by
    A. 1 1/2%   B. 2%   C. 1%   D. 3/4 1/4

55. The seniority score of Brown is
    A. equal to Hunt's
    B. twice Hunt's
    C. more than Hunt's by 1 1/2%
    D. less than Hunt's by 1/2%

56. Green's efficiency score is
    A. twice that of Kane
    B. equal to that of Kane
    C. less than Kane's by 1/2%
    D. less than Kane's by 1%

57. Of the following employees, the one who has the LOWEST efficiency score is
    A. Brown   B. Fox   C. Hunt   D. Kane

58. A comparison of Hunt's efficiency score with his seniority score reveals that his efficiency score is
    A. less than his seniority score by 1/2%
    B. less than his seniority score by 3/4%
    C. equal to his seniority score
    D. greater than his seniority score by 1/2%

59. Fox's service rating is
    A. 72 1/2%   B. 74%   C. 76 1/2%   D. 76 3/4%

60. Brown's service rating is
    A. less than 78%
    B. 78%
    C. 78 1/4%
    D. more than 78 1/4%

61. Cole's service rating exceeds Kane's by
    A. less than 2%
    B. 2%
    C. 2 1/4%
    D. more than 2 1/4%

Questions 62-71.

DIRECTIONS: Each of the sentences numbered 62 to 71 may be classified under one of the following four options:
(A) faulty; contains an error in grammar only
(B) faulty; contains an error in spelling only
(C) faulty; contains an error in grammar and an error in spelling
(D) correct; contains no error in grammar or in spelling

Examine each sentence carefully to determine under which of the above four options it is best classified. Then, in the correspondingly numbered space at the right, write the letter preceding the option which is the BEST of the four listed above.

62. A recognized principle of good management is that an assignment should be given to whomever is best qualified to carry it out. 62._____

63. He considered it a privilege to be allowed to review and summarize the technical reports issued annually by your agency. 63._____

64. Because the warehouse was in an inaccessable location, deliveries of electric fixtures from the warehouse were made only in large lots. 64._____

65. Having requisitioned the office supplies, Miss Brown returned to her desk and resumed the computation of petty cash disbursements. 65._____

66. One of the advantages of this chemical solution is that records treated with it are not inflammable. 66._____

67. The complaint of this employee, in addition to the complaints of the other employees, were submitted to the grievance committee. 67._____

68. A study of the duties and responsibilities of each of the various categories of employees was conducted by an unprejudiced classification analyst. 68._____

69. Ties of friendship with this subordinate compels him to withold the censure that the subordinate deserves. 69._____

70. Neither of the agencies are affected by the decision to institute a program for rehabilitating physically handicaped men and women. 70._____

71. The chairman stated that the argument between you and he was creating an intolerable situation. 71._____

Questions 72-75.

DIRECTIONS: Each of Questions 72 through 75 consists of a statement containing five words in capital letters. One of these capitalized words is not in keeping with the meaning which the statement is evidently intended to convey. The five words in capital letters in each statement are reprinted after the statement. In the correspondingly numbered space at the right, write the letter preceding the one of the five words which does MOST to spoil the true meaning of the statement.

72. The alert employee will find, EVEN in the best managed offices, violations of some of the rules of good office management. However, further study will reveal that the correction of such violations is by ALL means a SIMPLE matter, BUT requires research, time, patience, and often a high degree of MANAGERIAL ability. 72._____

    A. Even   B. All   C. Simple   D. But   E. Managerial

73. The information clerk in any organization must DELEGATE tact, courtesy, and good judgment in DEALING with callers, many of whom, on the other hand, DISREGARD business ETIQUETTE in their CONTACT with the information clerk. 73._____

    A. Delegate   B. Dealing   C. Disregard
    D. Etiquette   E. Contact

74. When the supervisor gives advancement or other rewards only to SUBORDINATES who have REQUESTED them, or shows a sincere INTEREST in the welfare of his staff, he is building FAVORABLE ATTITUDES.

    A. Subordinates   B. Requested   C. Interest
    D. Favorable   E. Attitudes

75. An appointee to the City's civil service must be a bona fide resident of the City for at least three years immediately prior to his APPOINTMENT. An appointee who served in the Armed Forces retains as his legal address that place where he resided prior to his ENTRY into the MILITARY service, PROVIDED he has taken definite action to establish a new RESIDENCE.

    A. Appointment   B. Entry   C. Military
    D. Provided   E. Residence

KEY (CORRECT ANSWERS)

1. D	16. D	31. B	46. D	61. A
2. B	17. C	32. D	47. C	62. A
3. B	18. B	33. C	48. A	63. D
4. A	19. C	34. A	49. A	64. B
5. C	20. D	35. D	50. C	65. D
6. A	21. D	36. B	51. D	66. B
7. C	22. C	37. A	52. B	67. A
8. B	23. A	38. B	53. A	68. D
9. A	24. B	39. C	54. C	69. C
10. D	25. A	40. C	55. B	70. C
11. B	26. B	41. A	56. C	71. A
12. C	27. B	42. D	57. B	72. B
13. A	28. D	43. A	58. D	73. A
14. B	29. A	44. D	59. D	74. B
15. D	30. C	45. B	60. B	75. D

EXAMINATION SECTION
TEST 1

DIRECTIONS: Each question or incomplete statement is followed by several suggested answers or completions. Select the one that BEST answers the question or completes the statement. *PRINT THE LETTER OF THE CORRECT ANSWER IN THE SPACE AT THE RIGHT.*

1. A multi-line telephone with buttons for eight separate lines, plus a *hold* button, is often used when an office requires more than one outside line.
   If you are talking on one line of this type of office phone when another call comes in, what is the procedure to follow if you want to answer the second call but keep the first call on the line?
   Push the
   A. *hold* button at the same time as you push the *pickup* button of the ringing line
   B. *hold* button and then push the *pickup* button of the ringing line
   C. *pickup* button of the ringing line and then push the *hold* button
   D. *pickup* button of the ringing line and push the *hold* button when you return to the original line

   1._____

2. Suppose that you are asked to prepare a petty cash statement for March. The original and one copy are to go to the personnel office. One copy is to go to the fiscal office, and another copy is to go to your supervisor. The last copy is for your files.
   In preparing the statement and the copies, how many sheets of copy paper should you use?
   A. 3   B. 4   C. 5   D. 8

   2._____

3. Which one of the following is the LEAST important advantage of putting the subject of a letter in the heading to the right of the address? It
   A. makes filing of the copy easier
   B. makes more space available in the body of the letter
   C. simplifies distribution of letters
   D. simplifies determination of the subject of the letter

   3._____

4. Of the following, the MOST efficient way to put 100 copies of a one-page letter into 9½" x 4⅛" envelopes for mailing is to fold _____ into an envelope.
   A. each letter and insert it immediately after folding
   B. each letter separately until all 100 are folded; then insert each one
   C. the 100 letters two at a time, then separate them and insert each one
   D. two letters together, slip them apart, and insert each one

   4._____

17

5. When preparing papers for filing, it is NOT desirable to
   A. smooth papers that are wrinkled
   B. use paper clips to keep related papers together in the files
   C. arrange the papers in the order in which they will be filed
   D. mend torn papers with cellophane tape

6. Of the following, the BEST reason for a clerical unit to have its own duplicating machine is that the unit
   A. uses many forms which it must reproduce internally
   B. must make two copies of each piece of incoming mail for a special file
   C. must make seven copies of each piece of outgoing mail
   D. must type 200 envelopes each month for distribution to the same offices

7. Several offices use the same photocopying machine.
   If each office must pay its share of the cost of running this machine, the BEST way of determining how much of this cost should be charged to each of these offices is to
   A. determine the monthly number of photocopies made by each office
   B. determine the monthly number of originals submitted for photocopying by each office
   C. determine the number of times per day each office uses the photocopying machine
   D. divide the total cost of running the photocopy machine by the total number of offices using the machine

8. Which one of the following would it be BEST to use to indicate that a file folder has been removed from the files for temporary use in another office?
   A(n)
   A. cross-reference card   B. tickler file marker
   C. aperture card   D. out guide

9. Which one of the following is the MOST important objective of filing?
   A. Giving a secretary something to do in her spare time
   B. Making it possible to locate information quickly
   C. Providing a place to store unneeded documents
   D. Keeping extra papers from accumulating on workers' desks

10. If a check has been made out for an incorrect amount, the BEST action for the writer of the check to take is to
    A. erase the original amount and enter the correct amount
    B. cross out the original amount with a single line and enter the correct amount above it
    C. black out the original amount so that it cannot be read and enter the correct amount above it
    D. write a new check

11. Which one of the following BEST describes the usual arrangement of a tickler file?
    A. Alphabetical
    B. Chronological
    C. Numerical
    D. Geographical

11.____

12. Which one of the following is the LEAST desirable filing practice?
    A. Using staples to keep papers together
    B. Filing all material without regard to date
    C. Keeping a record of all materials removed from the files
    D. Writing filing instructions on each paper prior to filing

12.____

13. Assume that one of your duties is to keep records of the office supplies used by your unit for the purpose of ordering new supplies when the old supplies run out.
    The information that will be of MOST help in letting you know when to reorder supplies is the
    A. quantity issued
    B. quantity received
    C. quantity on hand
    D. stock number

13.____

Questions 14-19.

DIRECTIONS: Questions 14 through 19 consist of sets of names and addresses. In each question, the name and address in Column II should be an exact copy of the name and address in Column I. If there is
a mistake *only* in the name, mark your answer A;
a mistake *only* in the address, mark your answer B;
a mistake in *both* name and address, mark your answer C;
no mistake in either name or address, mark your answer D.

SAMPLE QUESTION

Column I
Michael Filbert
456 Reade Street
New York, N.Y. 10013

Column II
Michael Filbert
645 Reade Street
New York, N.Y. 10013

Since there is a mistake only in the address (the street number should be 456 instead of 645), the answer to the sample question is B.

COLUMN I

COLUMN II

14. Esta Wong
    141 West 68 St.
    New York, N.Y. 10023

    Esta Wang
    141 West 68 St.
    New York,, N.Y. 10023

14.____

15. Dr. Alberto Grosso
    3475 12th Avenue
    Brooklyn, N.Y. 11218

    Dr. Alberto Grosso
    3475 12th Avenue
    Brooklyn, N.Y. 11218

15.____

	Column I	Column II	
16.	Mrs. Ruth Bortlas 482 Theresa Ct. Far Rockaway, N.Y. 11691	Ms. Ruth Bortlas 482 Theresa Ct. Far Rockaway, N.Y. 11169	16.____
17.	Mr. and Mrs. Howard Fox 2301 Sedgwick Avenue Bronx, N.Y. 10468	Mr. and Mrs. Howard Fox 231 Sedgwick Ave. Bronx, N.Y. 10458	17.____
18.	Miss Marjorie Black 223 East 23 Street New York, N.Y. 10010	Miss Margorie Black 223 East 23 Street New York, N.Y. 10010	18.____
19.	Michelle Herman 806 Valley Rd. Old Tappan, N.J. 07675	Michelle Hermann 806 Valley Dr. Old Tappan, N.J. 07675	19.____

Questions 20-25.

DIRECTIONS: Questions 20 through 25 are to be answered SOLELY on the basis of the information in the following passage.

Basic to every office is the need for proper lighting. Inadequate lighting is a familiar cause of fatigue and serves to create a somewhat dismal atmosphere in the office. One requirement of proper lighting is that it be of an appropriate intensity. Intensity is measured in foot-candles. According to the Illuminating Engineering Society of New York, for casual seeing tasks such as in reception rooms, inactive file rooms, and other service areas, it is recommended that the amount of light be 30 foot-candles. For ordinary seeing tasks such as reading and work in active file rooms and in mail rooms, the recommended lighting is 100 foot-candles. For very difficult seeing tasks such as accounting, transcribing, and business machine use, the recommended lighting is 150 foot-candles.

Lighting intensity is only one requirement. Shadows and glare are to be avoided. For example, the larger the proportion of a ceiling filled with lighting units, the more glare-free and comfortable the lighting will be. Natural lighting from windows is not too dependable because on dark wintry days, windows yield little usable light, and on sunny afternoons, the glare from windows may be very distracting. Desks should not face the windows. Finally, the main lighting source ought to be overhead and to the left of the user.

20. According to the above passage, insufficient light in the office may cause 20.____
    A. glare   B. shadows   C. tiredness   D. distraction

21. Based on the above passage, which of the following must be considered when planning lighting arrangements? 21.____
The
    A. amount of natural light present
    B. amount of work to be done
    C. level of difficulty of work to be done
    D. type of activity to be carried out

5 (#1)

22. It can be inferred from the above passage that a well-coordinated lighting scheme is LIKELY to result in
    A. greater employee productivity
    B. elimination of light reflection
    C. lower lighting cost
    D. more use of natural light

22._____

23. Of the following, the BEST title for the above passage is
    A. Characteristics of Light
    B. Light Measurement Devices
    C. Factors to Consider When Planning Lighting Systems
    D. Comfort vs. Cost When Devising Lighting Arrangements

23._____

24. According to the above passage, a foot-candle is a measurement of the
    A. number of bulbs used
    B. strength of the light
    C. contrast between glare and shadow
    D. proportion of the ceiling filled with lighting units

24._____

25. According to the above passage, the number of foot-candles of light that would be needed to copy figures onto a payroll is _____ foot-candles.
    A. less than 30   B. 30   C. 100   D. 150

25._____

KEY (CORRECT ANSWERS)

1.	B	11.	B
2.	B	12.	B
3.	B	13.	C
4.	A	14.	A
5.	B	15.	D
6.	A	16.	C
7.	A	17.	B
8.	D	18.	A
9.	B	19.	C
10.	D	20.	C

21. D
22. A
23. C
24. B
25. D

TEST 2

DIRECTIONS: Each question or incomplete statement is followed by several suggested answers or completions. Select the one that BEST answers the question or completes the statement. *PRINT THE LETTER OF THE CORRECT ANSWER IN THE SPACE AT THE RIGHT.*

1. Assume that a supervisor has three subordinates who perform clerical tasks. One of the employees retires and is replaced by someone who is transferred from another unit in the agency. The transferred employee tells the supervisor that she has worked as a clerical employee for two years and understands clerical operations quite well. The supervisor then assigns the transferred employee to a desk, tells the employee to begin working, and returns to his own desk.
   The supervisor's action in this situation is
   A. *proper;* experienced clerical employees do not require training when they are transferred to new assignments
   B. *improper;* before the supervisor returns to his desk, he should tell the other two subordinates to watch the transferred employee perform the work
   C. *proper;* if the transferred employee makes any mistakes, she will bring them to the supervisor's attention
   D. *improper;* the supervisor should find out what clerical tasks the transferred employee has performed and give her instruction in those which are new or different

1.____

2. Assume that you are falling behind in completing your work assignments and you believe that your workload is too heavy.
   Of the following, the BEST course of action for you to take FIRST is to
   A. discuss the problem with your supervisor
   B. decide which of your assignments can be postponed
   C. try to get some of your co-workers to help you out
   D. plan to take some of the work home with you in order to catch up

2.____

3. Suppose that one of the clerks under your supervision is filling in monthly personnel forms. She asks you to explain a particular personnel regulation which is related to various items on the forms. You are not thoroughly familiar with the regulation.
   Of the following responses you may make, the one which will gain the MOST respect from the clerk and which is generally the MOST advisable is to
   A. tell the clerk to do the best she can and that you will check her work later
   B. inform the clerk that you are not sure of a correct explanation but suggest a procedure for her to follow
   C. give the clerk a suitable interpretation so that she will think you are familiar with all regulations
   D. tell the clerk that you will have to read the regulation more thoroughly before you can give her an explanation

3.____

4. Charging out records until a specified due date, with prompt follow-up if they are not returned, is a
   A. *good* idea; it may prevent the records from being kept needlessly on someone's desk for long periods of time
   B. *good* idea; it will indicate the extent of your authority to other departments
   C. *poor* idea; the person borrowing the material may make an error because of the pressure put upon him to return the records
   D. *poor* idea; other departments will feel that you do not trust them with the records and they will be resentful

4.____

Questions 5-9.

DIRECTIONS: Questions 5 through 9 consist of three lines of code letters and numbers. The numbers on each line should correspond with the code letters on the same line in accordance with the table below.

Code Letter	P	L	I	J	B	O	H	U	C	G
Corresponding Letter	0	1	2	3	4	5	6	7	8	9

On some of the lines, an error exists in the coding. Compare the letters and numbers in each question carefully. If you find an error or errors on
 only one of the lines in the question, mark your answer A;
 any two lines in the question, mark your answer B;
 all three lines in the question, mark your answer C;
 none of the lines in the question, mark your answer D.

SAMPLE QUESTION
JHOILCP   3652180
BICLGUP   4286970
UCIBHLJ   5824613

In the above sample, the first line is correct since each code letter listed has the correct corresponding number. On the second line, an error exists because code letter L should have the number 1 instead of the number 6. On the third line, an error exists because the code letter U should have the number 7 instead of the number 5. Since there are errors on two of the three lines, the correct answer is B.

5. BULJCIP   4713920
   HIGPOUL   6290571
   OCUHJJBI   5876342

5.____

6. CUBLOIJ   8741023
   LCLGCLB   1818914
   JPUHIOC   3076158

6.____

7. OIJGCBPO   52398405
   UHPBLIOP   76041250
   CLUIPGPC   81720908

7.____

8. BPCOUOJI   40875732
    UOHCIPLB   75682014
    GLHUUCBJ   92677843

9. HOIOHJLH   65256361
    IOJJHHBP   25536640
    OJHBJOPI   53642502

Questions 10-13.

DIRECTIONS: Questions 10 through 13 are to be answered SOLELY on the basis of the information given in the following passage.

The mental attitude of the employee toward safety is exceedingly important in preventing accidents. All efforts designed to keep safety on the employee's mind and to keep accident prevention a live subject in the office will help substantially in a safety program. Although it may seem strange, it is common for people to be careless. Therefore, safety education is a continuous process.

Safety rules should be explained, and the reasons for their rigid enforcement should be given to employees. Telling employees to be careful or giving similar general safety warnings and slogans is probably of little value. Employees should be informed of basic safety fundamentals. This can be done through staff meetings, informal suggestions to employees, movies, and safety instruction cards. Safety instruction cards provide the employees with specific suggestions about safety and serve as a series of timely reminder helping to keep safety on the minds of employees. Pictures, posters, and cartoon sketches on bulletin boards that are located in areas continually used by employees arouse the employees' interest in safety. It is usually good to supplement this type of safety promotion with intensive individual follow-up.

10. The above passage implies that the LEAST effective of the following safety measures is
    A. rigid enforcement of safety rules
    B. getting employees to think in terms of safety
    C. elimination of unsafe conditions in the office
    D. telling employees to stay alert at all times

11. The reason given by the passage for maintaining ongoing safety education is that
    A. people are often careless
    B. office tasks are often dangerous
    C. the value of safety slogans increases with repetition
    D. safety rules change frequently

12. Which one of the following safety aids is MOST likely to be preferred by the passage? A
    A. cartoon of a man tripping over a carton and yelling, *Keep aisles clear!*
    B. poster with a large number one and a caption saying, *Safety First*

C. photograph of a very neatly arranged office
D. large sign with the word THINK in capital letters

13. Of the following, the BEST title for the above passage is 13._____
    A. Basic Safety Fundamentals
    B. Enforcing Safety Among Careless Employees
    C. Attitudes Toward Safety
    D. Making Employees Aware of Safety

Questions 14-21.

DIRECTIONS: Questions 14 through 21 are to be answered SOLELY on the basis of the information and chart given below.

The following chart shows expenses in five selected categories for a one-year period, expressed as percentages of these same expenses during the previous year. The chart compares two different offices. In Office T (represented by ▓▓▓▓), a cost reduction program has been tested for the past year. The other office, Office Q (represented by ////), served as a control, in that no special effort was made to reduce costs during the past year.

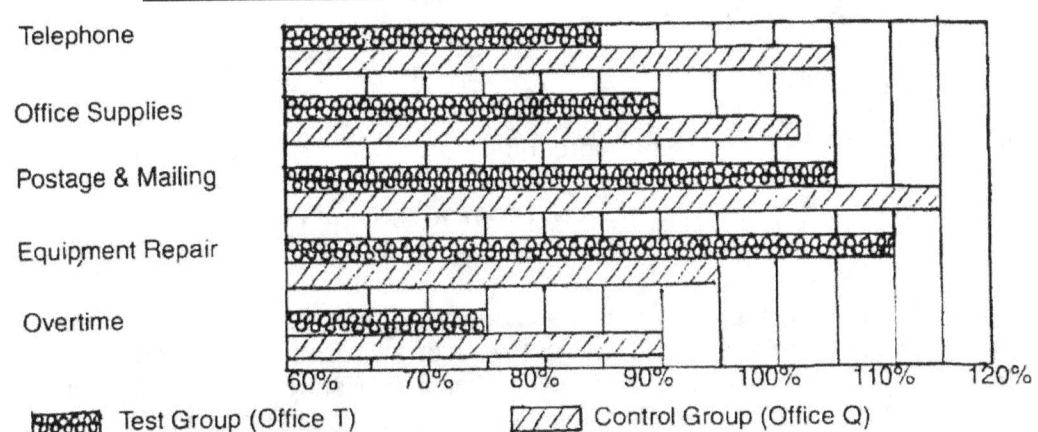

14. In Office T, which category of expense showed the greatest percentage REDUCTION from 2019 to 2020? 14._____
    A. Telephone   B. Office Supplies
    C. Postage & Mailing   D. Overtime

15. In which expense category did Office T show the BEST results in percentage terms when compared to Office Q? 15._____
    A. Telephone   B. Office Supplies
    C. Postage & Mailing   D. Overtime

16. According to the above chart, the cost reduction program was LEAST effective for the expense category of
    A. Office Supplies
    B. Postage & Mailing
    C. Equipment Repair
    D. Overtime

17. Office T's telephone costs went down during 2020 by approximately how many percentage points?
    A. 15
    B. 20
    C. 85
    D. 104

18. Which of the following changes occurred in expenses for Office Supplies in Office Q in the year 2020 as compared with the year 2019?
    They
    A. increased by more than 100%
    B. remained the same
    C. decreased by a few percentage points
    D. increased by a few percentage points

19. For which of the following expense categories do the results in Office T and the results in Office Q differ MOST NEARLYY by 10 percentage points?
    A. Telephone
    B. Postage & Mailing
    C. Equipment Repair
    D. Overtime

20. In which expense category did Office Q's costs show the GREATEST percentage increase in 2020?
    A. Telephone
    B. Office Supplies
    C. Postage & Mailing
    D. Equipment Repair

21. In Office T, by approximately what percentage did overtime expense change during the past year? It
    A. *increased* by 15%
    B. *increased* by 75%
    C. *decreased* by 10%
    D. *decreased* by 25%

22. In a particular agency, there were 160 accidents in 2017. Of these accidents, 75% were due to unsafe acts and the rest were due to unsafe conditions. In the following year, a special safety program was established. The number of accidents in 2019 due to unsafe acts was reduced to 35% of what it had been in 2017.
    How many accidents due to unsafe acts were there in 2019?
    A. 20
    B. 36
    C. 42
    D. 56

23. At the end of every month, the petty cash fund of Agency A is reimbursed for payments made from the fund during the month. During the month of February, the amounts paid from the fund were entered on receipts as follows: 10 bus fares of $3.50 each and one taxi fare of $35.00. At the end of the month, the money left in the fund was in the following denominations: 15 ten-dollar bills, 10 one-dollar bills, 40 quarters, and 100 dimes.
    If the petty cash fund is reduced by 20% for the following month, how much money will there be available in the petty cash fund for March?
    A. $110.00
    B. $200.00
    C. $215.00
    D. $250.00

24. The one of the following records which it would be MOST advisable to keep in alphabetical order is a
    A. continuous listing of phone messages, including time and caller, for your supervisor
    B. listing of individuals currently employed by your agency in a particular title
    C. record of purchases paid for by the petty cash fund
    D. dated record of employees who have borrowed material from the files in your office

25. Assume that you have been asked to copy by hand a column of numbers with two decimal places from one record to another. Each number consists of three, four, and five digits.
    In order to copy them quickly and accurately, you should copy
    A. each number exactly, making sure that the column of digits farthest to the right is in a straight line and all other columns are lined up
    B. the column of digits farthest to the right and then copy the next column of digits moving from right to left
    C. the column of digits farthest to the left and then copy the next column of digits moving from left to right
    D. the digits to the right of each decimal point and then copy the digits to the left of each decimal point

KEY (CORRECT ANSWERS)

1.	D	11.	A
2.	A	12.	A
3.	D	13.	D
4.	A	14.	D
5.	A	15.	A
6.	C	16.	C
7.	D	17.	A
8.	B	18.	D
9.	C	19.	B
10.	D	20.	C

21.	D
22.	C
23.	B
24.	B
25.	A

EXAMINATION SECTION
TEST 1

DIRECTIONS: Each question or incomplete statement is followed by several suggested answers or completions. Select the one that BEST answers the question or completes the statement. *PRINT THE LETTER OF THE CORRECT ANSWER IN THE SPACE AT THE RIGHT.*

1. As head of the filing unit in your department, you have been receiving complaints that material which should be in the files cannot be located. On investigating this matter, you find that one of your new clerks has been careless in placing material in the files.
   The BEST of the following actions which you might take FIRST is to

   A. admonish this clerk and tell him that he will be given a below-average service rating if his carelessness continues
   B. remind this clerk that he is a probationary employee and that his services may be terminated at the end of his probationary period if his carelessness continues
   C. call the attention of this clerk to the effects of filing and impress upon him the necessity for accuracy in filing
   D. give this clerk another assignment in the unit where accuracy is less essential

2. The GREATEST amount of improvement in the efficiency and morale of a unit will be brought about by the supervisor who

   A. reminds his employees constantly that they must follow departmental regulations
   B. frequently praises an employee in the presence of the other employees in the unit
   C. invariably gives mild reproof and constructive criticism to subordinates when he discovers that they have made a mistake
   D. assigns duties to employees in conformance with their abilities and interests as far as practicable

3. Assume that you are the supervisor of a unit which performs routine clerical work. For you to encourage your subordinates to make suggestions for increasing the efficiency of the unit is

   A. *undesirable;* employees who perform routine work may resent having additional duties and responsibilities assigned to them
   B. *desirable;* by presenting criticism of each other's work, the employees may develop a competitive spirit and in this way increase their efficiency
   C. *undesirable;* the employees may conclude that the supervisor is not capable of efficiently supervising the work of the unit
   D. *desirable;* increased interest in their assignment may be acquired by the employees, and the work of the unit may be performed more efficiently

4. The MOST accurate of the following statements regarding the chief purpose for maintaining a perpetual inventory of office supplies is that it

   A. eliminates the necessity for making a physical inventory of office supplies
   B. makes available at all times a record of the balance of office supplies on hand
   C. reduces the amount of clerical work required in distributing supplies
   D. reduces the amount of paper work involved in requisitioning supplies

5. Of the following, a centralized filing system is LEAST suitable for filing

   A. material which is confidential in nature
   B. routine correspondence
   C. periodic reports of the divisions of the department
   D. material used by several divisions of the department

6. Form letters should be used mainly when

   A. an office has to reply to a great many similar inquiries
   B. the type of correspondence varies widely
   C. it is necessary to have letters which are well-phrased and grammatically correct
   D. letters of inquiry have to be answered as soon as possible after they are received

7. Assume that you have recommended that one of your subordinates be given a below-average service rating. The subordinate disagreed with your recommendation and requests that you discuss the service rating report with him.
In taking up this matter with the employee, the BEST of the following procedures for you to follow is to

   A. discuss the general standards of evaluation you have used, rather than his specific deficiencies
   B. tell him that it would be too time-consuming to discuss his report with him, but inform him that objective standards were used in evaluating all employees and that the reports will be reviewed by an impartial board which will make any changes it deems necessary
   C. explain the standards of evaluation you have used and discuss this subordinate's work with him in relation to these standards
   D. point out to your subordinate that you are in a better position than he to compare his work with that of the other employees in your unit

8. Suppose that you are assigned to prepare a form from which certain information will be posted in a ledger. It would be MOST helpful to the person posting the information in the ledger if, in designing the form, you were to

   A. use the same color paper for both the form and the ledger
   B. make the form the same size as the pages of the ledger
   C. have the information on the form in the same order as that used in the ledger
   D. include in the form a box which is to be initialed when the data on the form have been posted in the ledger

9. A misplaced record is a lost record.
Of the following, the MOST valid implication of this statement in regard to office work is that

   A. all records in an office should be filed in strict alphabetical order
   B. accuracy in filing is essential
   C. only one method of filing should be used throughout the office
   D. files should be locked when not in use

10. John Smith is applying for a provisional appointment as a clerk in your department. He presents a letter of recommendation from a former employer stating: *John Smith was rarely late or absents he has a very pleasing manner, and never got into an argument with his fellow employees.*
The above information concerning this applicant

   A. proves clearly that he produces more work than the average employee
   B. indicates that he was probably attempting to conceal his inefficiency from his former employer
   C. presents no conclusive evidence of his ability to do clerical work
   D. indicates clearly that with additional training he will make a good supervisor

11. It is not possible to draw a hard and fast line between training courses for greater efficiency on the present job.
This statement means MOST NEARLY that

   A. to be worthwhile, a training course should prepare the employee for promotion as well as for greater efficiency on the present job
   B. training courses should be designed only to increase employee efficiency on the present job
   C. training courses should be given only to employees who are competing for promotion
   D. by attending a training course for promotion, employees may become more efficient in their present work

12. Approximate figures serve as well as exact figures to indicate trends and make comparisons.
Of the following, the MOST accurate statement on the basis of this statement is that

   A. it takes less time to obtain approximate figures than exact figures
   B. exact figures are rarely used as they require too much computation
   C. for certain purposes, approximate figures are as revealing as exact figures
   D. approximate figures can usually be used in place of exact figures

13. Suppose that you are placed in charge of a unit in your department. You find that many of the employees have been disregarding the staff regulation requiring employees to be at their desks at 9:05 A.M.
Of the following, the LEAST desirable course of action for you to take would be to

   A. call a meeting of the staff and explain why it is essential that all employees be at their desks at 9:05 A.M.
   B. post conspicuously on the bulletin board a notice calling the employees' attention to the frequent violation of this regulation and requesting them to observe this regulation
   C. recommend an above-average service rating for all employees who consistently comply with this regulation, provided their work is satisfactory
   D. summon the offenders and explain to them how their violation of this regulation results in decreasing the efficiency of the unit

14. Suppose that certain office responsibilities require you to be frequently absent from the unit you supervise. You have, therefore, decided to designate one of your staff members to act as unit head in your absence.
    Of the following factors, the one which is MOST important in selecting the employee best fitted for this assignment is his

    A. manner and personal appearance
    B. estimated ability to perform work of a supervisory nature
    C. ability to perform his present duties
    D. relative seniority in the service

15. One of the assignments in the unit you supervise is the checking of a list of 500 unalphabetized names against an alphabetical 5x8 card index containing several thousand names. The clerk performing this task is to make sure that there is a card in the file for each name on the list.
    The one of the following which you should suggest as the BEST procedure for the clerk to follow is for him to

    A. rewrite the names on the list in alphabetical order, look for the corresponding card in the file, and place a check mark next to each name on the list for which he finds a card
    B. take each name on the list in turn, look for the corresponding card in the file, and place a check mark in the corner of each card he finds
    C. go through all the cards in the file in consecutive order and place a check mark next to each name on the list for which he finds a card
    D. take each name on the list in turn, look for the corresponding card in the file, and place a check mark next to each name on the list for which he finds a card

16. Suppose that you are in charge of a unit which maintains a rather intricate filing system. A new file clerk has been added to your staff.
    Of the following assignments that may be given to this clerk, the one which requires the LEAST amount of knowledge of the filing system is

    A. placing material in the files
    B. removing papers from the files
    C. classifying and coding material for filing
    D. keeping a record of material taken from, and returned to, the files

17. In undertaking to improve the method of performing a certain job or operation, the new office manager should first ascertain the

    A. present method of performing the job
    B. purpose of the job
    C. number and titles of employees assigned to the job
    D. methods used by other agencies to perform the same kind of job

18. The proofreading of a large number of papers has been assigned to two clerks. These clerks have been instructed to indicate all necessary corrections on a slip of paper, attach this correction slip to the papers, and send them to the typist for correction.
    Of the following additional steps that might be taken before sending the papers to the xerox operator, the BEST one is that the

A. clerks should proofread each paper in its entirety after the corrections have been made on it
B. typist should make the necessary corrections and return the correction slip and the corrected papers to the clerks; the clerks should then examine the papers to see that all the requested corrections have been made properly
C. typist should make the necessary corrections, placing a check mark opposite each correction noted on the correction slip; she should then review the correction slip to make sure that no correction has been omitted
D. typist should make the necessary corrections, place a check mark opposite each correction noted on the correction slip, and return the papers and the correction slip to the clerks; the clerks should then review the correction slip to make sure that a check mark has been placed opposite each item on the correction slip

19. Suppose you are the supervisor of a unit in a department. You notice that a clerk with long service in the department is arguing with a recently appointed clerk regarding the procedure to be followed in performing a certain task. Each is convinced he is right. The argument is disturbing the other employees.
Of the following, the BEST action for you to take in dealing with this problem is to

   A. call the clerks to your desk, discuss the matter with them, and then state which procedure is the correct one
   B. support the employee with the longer service, for to do otherwise will impair the morale of the office
   C. call the clerks to your desk and tell them to settle their differences without disturbing the others
   D. order the clerks to discontinue their argument immediately and to bring the matter up at the next staff conference, where the staff will determine which procedure is the correct one

20. Assume that you devised a new procedure which you expected would result in a substantial reduction in the amount of paper used in performing the work of the unit you supervise. After trying out this new procedure in your unit for several weeks, you find that the quantity of paper saved is considerably less than you anticipated.
Of the following, the BEST action for you to take first is to

   A. inform your staff that they are probably using paper unnecessarily, and that in view of the current paper shortage, you expect them to conserve paper as much as possible
   B. suspend the use of this new procedure until you can discover why it has not worked out as you anticipated
   C. invite your subordinates to submit suggestions as to how the procedure may be improved
   D. analyze the various processes involved in the new procedure to determine whether there are any factors which you may have overlooked

21. Assume that you are the head of the bureau of information in a department. You are faced with the problem of replacing the clerk assigned to the information desk.
Of the following available employees, the one who should be given the assignment is

A. John Jones, a new clerk who specialized in English at college and recently received a Master of Arts degree; at present, he has no permanent assignment
B. Mary Smith, an excellent stenographer who has had much experience as secretary to one of the bureau heads; she is intelligent, pleasant in manner, and learns quickly
C. Richard Roe, a clerk who has been rated as *tactful, dependable,* and *resourceful* by the various bureau heads who have prepared his service rating reports during the four years that he has been in the department
D. Jane Doe, who is a diligent typist when she works alone but who disturbs the other typists by her constant stream of chatter when she works near them

22. The one of the following which is the MOST accurate statement regarding routine operations in an office is that

    A. routine assignments should not last more than two or three days each week
    B. methods for performing routine work should be standardized as much as is practicable
    C. routine work performed by one employee should be checked by another employee
    D. changes in the procedures of a unit should not affect the existing routine operations of the unit

23. Modern management realizes the importance of sound personnel practices in business administration. It has found that production is largely dependent upon the effective utilization of an employee's interests, capabilities, and skills.
    Of the following, the MOST logical implication of the above statement is that

    A. there should be one bureau in each business organization to take charge of both production and personnel administration
    B. production cannot be increased without the utilization of a sound personnel policy
    C. production will increase if the number of persons assigned to work in a business organization is increased
    D. maximum efficiency in an organization cannot be achieved without proper placement of employees

24. One of the stenographers under your supervision has completed all of her assignments, and there is no additional typing to be done.
    It would be LEAST desirable for you to suggest that she

    A. straighten up the supply cabinet to improve its appearance
    B. check the files for material that is surplus or outdated
    C. read the daily newspaper to keep up with current events
    D. practice shorthand or typing to improve her speed

25. Of the following, the BEST way for a supervisor to determine when further on-the-job training in a particular work area is needed is by

    A. evaluating the employees' work performance
    B. asking the employees
    C. determining the ratio of idle time to total work time
    D. classifying the jobs in the work area

Questions 26-30.

DIRECTIONS: Each of Questions 26 through 30 consists of a statement containing five words in capital letters. One of these words in capital letters is not in keeping with the meaning which the statement is evidently intended to carry. The five words in capital letters in each statement are reprinted after the statement. In the space at the right, write the letter preceding the one of the five words which does most to spoil the true meaning of the statement.

26. Within each major DIVISION in a properly set-up public or private organization, provision is made so that each NECESSARY activity is CARED for and lines of AUTHORITY and responsibility are clear-cut and INFINITE. 26._____

    A. division   B. necessary   C. cared
    D. authority   E. infinite

27. In public service, the scale of salaries paid must be INCIDENTAL to the services rendered, with due CONSIDERATION for the attraction of the desired MANPOWER and for the MAINTENANCE of a standard of living COMMENSURATE with the work to be performed. 27._____

    A. incidental   B. consideration   C. manpower
    D. maintenance   E. commensurate

28. An understanding of the AIMS of an organization by the staff will AID greatly in increasing the DEMAND of the correspondence work of the office, and will to a large extent DETERMINE the NATURE of the correspondence. 28._____

    A. aims   B. aid   C. demand
    D. determine   E. nature

29. BECAUSE the Civil Service Commission strongly feels that the MERIT system is a key factor in the MAINTENANCE of democratic government, it has adopted as one of its major DEFENSES the progressive democratization of its own PROCEDURES in dealing with candidates for positions in the public service. 29._____

    A. Because   B. merit   C. maintenance
    D. defenses   E. procedures

30. Retirement and pensions systems are ESSENTIAL not only to provide employees with a means of support in the future, but also to prevent longevity and CHARITABLE considerations from UPSETTING the PROMOTIONAL opportunities for RETIRED members of the career service. 30._____

    A. essential   B. charitable   C. upsetting
    D. promotional   E. retired

31. Suppose that the amount of money spent for supplies in 2005 for a division of a department was $15,650. This represented an increase of 12% over the amount spent for supplies for this division in 2004. The amount of money spent for supplies for this division in 2004 was MOST NEARLY 31._____

    A. $13,973   B. $13,772   C. $14,346   D. $13,872

32. Suppose that a group of five clerks have been assigned to insert 24,000 letters into envelopes. The clerks perform this work at the following rates of speed: Clerk A, 1100 letters an hour; Clerk B, 1450 letters an hour; Clerk C, 1200 letters an hour; Clerk D, 1300 letters an hour; Clerk E, 1250 letters an hour. At the end of two hours of work, Clerks C and D are assigned to another task. Fron the time that Clerks C and D were taken off the assignment, the number of hours required for the remaining clerks to complete this assignment is

    A. less than 3 hours
    B. 3 hours
    C. more than 3 hours, but less than 4 hours
    D. more than 4 hours

33. The employees were SKEPTICAL about the usefulness of the new procedure. The word *skeptical,* as used in this sentence, means MOST NEARLY

    A. enthusiastic   B. indifferent
    C. doubtful   D. misinformed

34. He presented ABSTRUSE reasons in defense of his proposal. The word *abstruse,* as used in this sentence, means MOST NEARLY

    A. unnecessary under the circumstances
    B. apparently without merit or value
    C. hard to be understood
    D. obviously sound

35. A program of AUSTERITY is in effect in many countries. The word *austerity,* as used in this sentence, means MOST NEARLY

    A. rigorous self-restraint   B. military censorship
    C. rugged individualism   D. self-indulgence

36. The terms of the contract were ABROGATED at the last meeting of the board. The *word abrogated,* as used in this sentence, means MOST NEARLY

    A. discussed   B. summarized
    C. agreed upon   D. annulled

37. The enforcement of STRINGENT regulations is a difficult task. The word *stringent,* as used in this sentence, means MOST NEARLY

    A. unreasonable   B. strict
    C. unpopular   D. obscure

38. You should not DISPARAGE the value of his suggestions. The word *disparage,* as used in this sentence, means MOST NEARLY

    A. ignore   B. exaggerate
    C. belittle   D. reveal

39. The employee's conduct was considered REPREHENSIBLE by his superior. The word *reprehensible,* as used in this sentence, means MOST NEARLY

A. worthy of reward or honor
B. in accordance with rules and regulations
C. detrimental to efficiency and morale
D. deserving of censure or rebuke

40. He said he would EMULATE the persistence of his co-workers. The word *emulate*, as used in this sentence, means MOST NEARLY

   A. strive to equal
   B. acknowledge
   C. encourage
   D. attach no significance to

40.____

41. The revised regulations on discipline contained several MITIGATING provisions. The word *mitigating*, as used in this sentence, means MOST NEARLY

   A. making more effective
   B. containing contradictions
   C. rendering less harsh
   D. producing much criticism

41.____

42. The arrival of the inspector at the office on that day was FORTUITOUS. The word *fortuitous*, as used in this sentence, means MOST NEARLY

   A. accidental
   B. unfortunate
   C. prearranged
   D. desirable

42.____

43. A clerk who comes across the abbreviation *et.al.* should know that it stands for

   A. for example
   B. and others
   C. disposition pending
   D. and every month thereafter

43.____

Questions 44-50.

DIRECTIONS: Questions 44 through 50 are to be answered SOLELY on the basis of the following information.

Assume that the following regulations were established in your department to compute vacation allowances for services rendered by its employees during the period from June 1, 2007 through May 31, 2008. You are to determine the answer to each of the questions on the basis of these regulations.

VACATION REGULATIONS
(For the Period June 1, 2007 - May 31, 2008)

The vacation allowance for this period is to be taken after May 31, 2008.

Standard Vacation Allowance
   Permanent per annum employees shall be granted 25 days vacation for a full year's service in such status. Employees who have served less than a full year in a permanent per annum status shall receive an allowance of 2 days for each month of such service.
   Per diem employees shall be granted 1 1/2 days vacation for each month of service in such status.
   Temporary employees shall be granted one day of vacation for each month of service in such status.

No vacation credit shall accrue to employees for the time they are on leave of absence.

Additional Allowance for Overtime

One day of vacation allowance shall be granted for each seven hours of accrued overtime. Where there is a balance of less than 7 hours of accrued overtime, one-half day of vacation shall be granted for each 3 1/2 hours of such overtime. In no case shall the additional vacation allowed for accrued overtime exceed 6 days.

Deductions for Excessive Sick Leave

Sick leave allowance for all employees, regardless of length of service, shall be 12 days for the year. Sick leave taken in excess of 12 days shall be deducted from vacation allowance. Any unused sick leave balance will be canceled on May 31, 2008.

Deductions for Excessive Lateness

Deductions for excessive lateness shall be made from vacation allowance in accordance with the following schedule:

No. of Times Late	Deduction from Vacation Allowance
0-50	no deduction
51-60	1/2 day
61-70	1 day
71-80	1 1/2 days
81-90	2 days
91-100	2 1/2 days
101-120	4 days
121-140	6 days
141 or over	penalty to be determined by Secretary of Department

Unused Vacation

Unused vacation allowance earned during the previous year shall be added to the current vacation allowance, up to a maximum of twelve days.

Note that the vacation allowances are for services rendered during the year ending May 31, 2008, and that computations for all employees are to be made as of that date.

44. Employee A served as a temporary employee from June 1, 2007 through January 31, 2008, and as a permanent per annum employee from February 1, 2008 through May 31, 2008. During the year, he accumulated 45 1/2 hours of overtime and was late 65 times. His vacation allowance should be _____ days.

   A. 16   B. 15   C. 21 1/2   D. 21

45. Employee B was newly appointed to the department as a per diem employee on September 1, 2007. During the year, he took 15 days of sick leave and was late 48 times. His vacation allowance should be _____ days.

| A. | less than 10 | B. | 10 1/2 |
| C. | 15 | D. | 12 1/2 |

46. Employee C has been a permanent per annum employee throughout the year. He had 15 days of vacation due him from the previous year. During the year, he was late 85 times, he took 10 days of sick leave, and he accumulated 38 1/2 hours of overtime.
His vacation allowance should be _____ days.

    A. 38 1/2   B. 42 1/2
    C. 40 1/2   D. more than 43

46._____

47. Employee D was newly appointed to the department as a permanent per annum employee on July 1, 2007. He was on leave of absence from December 1, 2007 through February 28, 2008. During the year, he took 6 days of sick leave, he was late 70 times, and he accumulated 21 hours of overtime.
His vacation allowance should be _____ days.

    A. 24   B. 18   C. 17 1/2   D. 19 1/2

47._____

48. Employee E served as a per diem employee from June 1, 2007 through July 31, 2007, and as a permanent per annum employee from August 1, 2007 to May 31, 2008. He had 6 days of vacation due him from the previous year. During the year, he took 13 days of sick leave, he accumulated 70 hours of overtime, and he was late 132 times.
His vacation allowance should be _____ days.

    A. less than 29   B. 29
    C. 30   D. more than 30

48._____

49. The maximum total vacation allowance which a permanent per annum employee can have due him by May 31, 2008 is _____ days.

    A. 43   B. 25   C. 31   D. 37

49._____

50. An employee who has served as a temporary employee for 6 months and as a permanent per annum employee for 6 months will earn exactly

    A. two-thirds as much vacation as an employee who has been on a permanent per annum basis for the whole year
    B. as much vacation as an employee who has been on a per diem basis for the whole year
    C. as much vacation as an employee who has been on a per diem basis for 4 months and on a permanent per annum basis for 8 months
    D. as much vacation as an employee who has been on a per diem basis for 8 months and on a permanent per annum basis for 5 months

50._____

Questions 51-60.

DIRECTIONS: Each of Questions 51 through 60 may be classified under one of the following four categories:

    A. faulty because of incorrect grammar or sentence structure
    B. faulty because of incorrect punctuation
    C. faulty because of incorrect spelling
    D. correct

Examine each sentence carefully to determine under which of the above four options it is best classified. Then, in the space at the right, write the letter preceding the option which is the BEST of the four suggested above. Each incorrect sentence contains but one type of error. Consider a sentence to be correct if it contains none of the types of errors mentioned, even though there may be other correct ways of expressing the same thought.

51. Although the department's supply of scratch pads and stationery have diminished considerably, the allotment for our division has not been reduced. 51.____

52. You have not told us whom you wish to designate as your secretary. 52.____

53. Upon reading the minutes of the last meeting, the new proposal was taken up for consideration. 53.____

54. Before beginning the discussion, we locked the door as a precautionery measure. 54.____

55. The supervisor remarked, "Only those clerks, who perform routine work, are permitted to take a rest period." 55.____

56. Not only will this duplicating machine make accurate copies, but it will also produce a quantity of work equal to fifteen transcribing typists. 56.____

57. "Mr. Jones," said the supervisor, "we regret our inability to grant you an extention of your leave of absence." 57.____

58. Although the employees find the work monotonous and fatigueing, they rarely complain. 58.____

59. We completed the tabulation of the receipts on time despite the fact that Miss Smith our fastest operator was absent for over a week. 59.____

60. The reaction of the employees who attended the meeting, as well as the reaction of those who did not attend, indicates clearly that the schedule is satisfactory to everyone concerned. 60.____

KEY (CORRECT ANSWERS)

1.	C	16.	D	31.	A	46.	C
2.	D	17.	B	32.	B	47.	B
3.	D	18.	B	33.	C	48.	A
4.	B	19.	A	34.	C	49.	A
5.	A	20.	D	35.	A	50.	B
6.	A	21.	C	36.	D	51.	A
7.	C	22.	B	37.	B	52.	D
8.	C	23.	D	38.	C	53.	A
9.	B	24.	C	39.	D	54.	C
10.	C	25.	A	40.	A	55.	B
11.	D	26.	E	41.	C	56.	A
12.	C	27.	A	42.	A	57.	C
13.	C	28.	C	43.	B	58.	C
14.	B	29.	D	44.	D	59.	B
15.	D	30.	E	45.	B	60.	D

42

EXAMINATION SECTION
TEST 1

DIRECTIONS: Each question or incomplete statement is followed by several suggested answers or completions. Select the one that BEST answers the question or completes the statement. *PRINT THE LETTER OF THE CORRECT ANSWER IN THE SPACE AT THE RIGHT.*

Questions 1-2.

DIRECTIONS: Questions 1 and 2 are to be answered on the basis of the following conditions.

Assume that you work for Department A, which occupies several floors in one building. There is a reception office on each floor. All visitors (persons not employed in the department) are required to go to the reception office on the same floor as the office of the person they want to see. They sign a register, their presence is announced by the receptionist, and they wait in the reception room for the person they are visiting.

1. As you are walking in the corridor of your department on your way to a meeting in Room 314, a visitor approaches you and asks you to direct her to Room 312. She says that she is delivering some papers to Mr. Crane in that office. The MOST APPROPRIATE action for you to take is to

    A. offer to deliver the papers to Mr. Crane since you will be passing his office
    B. suggest that she come with you since you will be passing Room 312
    C. direct her to the reception office where Mr. Crane will be contacted for her
    D. take her to the reception office and contact Mr. Crane for her

    1.____

2. You are acting as receptionist in the reception office on the second floor. A man enters, stating that he is an accountant from another department and that he has an appointment with Mr. Prince, who is located in Room 102 on the first floor.
The BEST action for you to take is to

    A. phone the reception office on the first floor and ask the receptionist to contact Mr. Prince
    B. advise the man to go to the reception office on the first floor where he will be further assisted
    C. contact Mr. Prince for him and ask that he come to your office where his visitor is waiting
    D. send him directly to Room 102 where he can see Mr. Prince

    2.____

3. One of the employees whom you supervise complains to you that you give her more work than the other employees and that she cannot finish these assignments by the time you expect them to be completed.
Of the following, the FIRST action you should then take is to

    A. tell the employee that you expect more work from her because the other employees do not have her capabilities
    B. assure the employee that you always divide the work equally among your subordinates

    3.____

C. review the employee's recent assignments in order to determine whether her complaint is justified
D. ask the employee if there are any personal problems which are interfering with the completion of the assignments

4. Assume that a staff regulation exists which requires an employee to inform his supervisor if the employee will be absent on a particular day.
If an employee fails to follow this regulation, the FIRST action his supervisor should take is to

   A. inform his own supervisor of the situation and ask for further instructions
   B. ask the employee to explain his failure to follow the regulation
   C. tell the employee that another breach of the regulation will lead to disciplinary action
   D. reprimand the employee for failing to follow the regulation

5. An employee tells his supervisor that he submitted an idea to the employees' suggestion program by mail over two months ago and still has not received an indication that the suggestion is being considered. The employee states that when one of his co-workers sent in a suggestion, he received a response within one week. The employee then asks his supervisor what he should do.
Which of the following is the BEST response for the supervisor to make?

   A. "Next time you have a suggestion, see me about it first and I will make sure that it is properly handled."
   B. "I'll try to find out whether your suggestion was received by the program and whether a response was sent."
   C. "Your suggestion probably wasn't that good so there's no sense in pursuing the matter any further."
   D. "Let's get together and submit the suggestion jointly so that it will carry more weight."

6. Assume that you have been trying to teach a newly appointed employee the filing procedures used in your office. The employee seems to be having difficulty learning the procedures even though you consider them relatively simple and you originally learned them in less time than you have already spent trying to teach the new employee.
Before you spend any time trying to teach him any new filing procedures, which of the following actions should you take FIRST?

   A. Try to teach him some other aspect of your office's work.
   B. Tell him that you had little difficulty learning the procedures and ask him why he finds them so hard to learn.
   C. Review with him those procedures you have tried to teach him and determine whether he understands them.
   D. Report to your supervisor that the new employee is unsuited for the work performed in your office.

7. There is a rule in your office that all employees must sign in and out for lunch. You notice that a new employee who is under your direct supervision has not signed in or out for lunch for the past three days. Of the following, the MOST effective action to take is to

A. immediately report this matter to your supervisor
B. note this infraction of rules on the employee's personnel record
C. remind the employee that she must sign in and out for lunch every day
D. send around a memorandum to all employees in the office telling them they must sign in and out for lunch every day

Questions 8-15.

DIRECTIONS: Questions 8 through 15 each show in Column I names written on four cards (lettered w, x, y, z) which have to be filed. You are to choose the option (lettered A, B, C, or D) in Column II which BEST represents the proper order of filing according to the rules and sample question given below. The cards are to be filed according to the following Rules for Alphabetical Filing.

RULES FOR ALPHABETICAL FILING

Names of Individuals

1. The names of individuals are filed in strict alphabetical order, first according to the last name, then according to first name or initial, and finally according to middle name or initial. For example: George Allen precedes Edward Bell and Leonard Reston precedes Lucille Reston.

2. When last names are the same, for example, A. Green and Agnes Green, the one with the initial comes before the one with the name written out when the first initials are identical.

3. When first and last names are the same, a name without a middle initial comes before one with a middle initial. For example: Ralph Simon comes before both Ralph A. Simon and Ralph Adam Simon.

4. When first and last names are the same, a name with a middle initial comes before one with a middle name beginning with the same initial. For example: Sam P. Rogers comes before Sam Paul Rogers.

5. Prefixes such as De, O', Mac, Mc, and Van are filed as written and are treated as part of the names to which they are connected. For example: Gladys McTeaque is filed before Frances Meadows.

6. Abbreviated names are treated as if they were spelled out. For example: Chas. is filed as Charles and Thos. is filed as Thomas.

7. Titles and designations such as Dr., Mr., and Prof, are ignored in filing.

Names of Organizations

1. The names of business organizations are filed according to the order in which each word in the name appears. When an organization name bears the name of a person, it is filed according to the rules for filing names of people as given above. Vivian Quinn Boutique would, therefore, come before Security Locks Inc. because Quinn comes before Security.

4 (#1)

2. When numerals occur in a name, they are treated as if they were spelled out. For example: 4th Street Thrift Shop is filed as Fourth Street Thrift Shop.

3. When the following words are part of the name of an organization, they are ignored: on, the, of, and.

SAMPLE

	Column I	Column II	The correct way to file the cards is:
w.	Jane Earl	A. w, y, z, x	y. James Earl
x.	James A. Earle	B. y, w, z, x	w. Jane Earl
y.	James Earl	C. x, y, w, z	z. J. Earle
z.	J. Earle	D. x, w, y, z	x. James A. Earle

The correct filing order is shown by the letters, y, w, z, x (in that sequence). Since, in Column II, B appears in front of the letters, y, w, z, x (in that sequence), B is the correct answer to the sample question.

Now answer the following questions using that same procedure.

		Column I		Column II	
8.	w.	James Rothschild	A.	x, z, w, y	8.___
	x.	Julius B. Rothchild	B.	x, w, z, y	
	y.	B. Rothstein	C.	z, y, w, x	
	z.	Brian Joel Rothenstein	D.	z, w, x, y	
9.	w.	George S. Wise	A.	w, y, z, x	9.___
	x.	S. G. Wise	B.	x, w, y, z	
	y.	Geo. Stuart Wise	C.	y, x, w, z	
	z.	Prof. Diana Wise	D.	z, w, y, x	
10.	w.	10th Street Bus Terminal	A.	x, z, w, y	10.___
	x.	Buckingham Travel Agency	B.	y, x, w, z	
	y.	The Buckingham Theater	C.	w, z, y, x	
	z.	Burt Tompkins Studio	D.	x, w, y, z	
11.	w.	National Council of American Importers	A.	w, y, x, z	11.___
	x.	National Chain Co. of Providence	B.	x, z, w, y	
	y.	National Council on Alcoholism	C.	z, x, w, y	
	z.	National Chain Co.	D.	z, x, y, w	
12.	w.	Dr. Herbert Alvary	A.	w, y, x, z	12.___
	x.	Mr. Victor Alvarado	B.	z, w, x, y	
	y.	Alvar Industries	C.	y, z, x, w	
	z.	V. Alvarado	D.	w, z, x, y	

	Column I		Column II	
13.	w. Joan MacBride x. Wm. Mackey y. Roslyn McKenzie z. Winifred Mackey		A. w, x, z, y B. w, y, z, x C. w, z, x, y D. w, y, x, z	13._____

	Column I		Column II	
14.	w. 3 Way Trucking Co. x. 3rd Street Bakery y. 380 Realty Corp. z. Three Lions Pub		A. y, x, z, w B. y, z, w, x C. x, y, z, w D. x, y, w, z	14._____
15.	w. Miss Rose Leonard x. Rev. Leonard Lucas y. Sylvia Leonard Linen Shop z. Rose S. Leonard		A. z, w, x, y B. w, z, y, x C. w, x, z, y D. z, w, y, x	15._____

Questions 16-19.

DIRECTIONS: Answer Questions 16 through 19 ONLY on the basis of the information given in the following passage.

Work measurement concerns accomplishment or productivity. It has to do with results; it does not deal with the amount of energy used up, although in many cases this may be in direct proportion to the work output. Work measurement not only helps a manager to distribute work loads fairly, but it also enables him to define work sueeess in actual units, evaluate employee performance, and determine where corrective help is needed. Work measurement is accomplished by measuring the amount produced, measuring the time spent to produce it, and relating the two. To illustrate, it is common to speak of so many orders processed within a given time. The number of orders processed becomes meaningful when related to the amount of time taken.

Much of the work in an office can be measured fairly accurately and inexpensively. The extent of wo.rk measurement possible in any given case will depend upon the particular type of office tasks performed, but usually from two-thirds to three-fourths of all work in an office can be measured. It is true that difficulty in work measurement is encountered, for example, when the office work is irregular and not repeated often, or when the work is primarily mental rather than manual. These are problems, but they are used as excuses for doing no work measurement far more frequently than is justified.

16. According to the above passage, which of the following BEST illustrates the type of information obtained as a result of work measurement? A 16._____

   A. clerk takes one hour to file 150 folders
   B. typist types five letters
   C. stenographer works harder typing from shorthand notes than she does typing from a typed draft
   D. clerk keeps track of employees' time by computing sick leave, annual leave, and overtime leave

17. The above passage does NOT indicate that work measurement can be used to help a supervisor to determine

    A. why an employee is performing poorly on the job
    B. who are the fast and slow workers in the unit
    C. how the work in the unit should be divided up
    D. how long it should take to perform a certain task

18. According to the above passage, the kind of work that would be MOST difficult to measure would be such work as

    A. sorting mail
    B. designing a form for a new procedure
    C. photocopying various materials
    D. answering inquiries with form letters

19. The excuses mentioned in the above passage for failure to perform work measurement can be BEST summarized as the

    A. repetitive nature of office work
    B. costs involved in carrying out accurate work measurement
    C. inability to properly use the results obtained from work measurement
    D. difficulty involved in measuring certain types of work

Questions 20-24.

DIRECTIONS: In each of Questions 20 through 24, there is a sentence containing one underlined word. Choose the word (lettered A, B, C, or D) which means MOST NEARLY the same as the underlined word as it is used in the sentence.

20. Mr. Warren could not attend the luncheon because he had a prior appointment.

    A. conflicting   B. official
    C. previous   D. important

21. The time allowed to complete the task was not adequate.

    A. long   B. enough   C. excessive   D. required

22. The investigation unit began an extensive search for the information.

    A. complicated   B. superficial
    C. thorough   D. leisurely

23. The secretary answered the telephone in a courteous manner.

    A. businesslike   B. friendly
    C. formal   D. polite

24. The recipient of the money checked the total amount.

    A. receiver   B. carrier   C. borrower   D. giver

25. You receive a telephone call from an employee in another agency requesting information about a project being carried out by a division other than your own. You know little about the work being done, but you would like to help the caller.
Of the following, the BEST action for you to take is to

   A. ask the caller exactly what he would like to know and then tell him all you know about the work being done
   B. ask the caller to tell you exactly what he would like to know so that you can get the information while he waits
   C. tell the caller that you will have the call transferred to the division working on the project
   D. request that the caller write to you so that you can send him the necessary information

KEY (CORRECT ANSWERS)

1. C
2. B
3. C
4. B
5. B

6. C
7. C
8. A
9. D
10. B

11. D
12. C
13. A
14. C
15. B

16. A
17. A
18. B
19. D
20. C

21. B
22. C
23. D
24. A
25. C

TEST 2

DIRECTIONS: Each question or incomplete statement is followed by several suggested answers or completions. Select the one that BEST answers the question or completes the statement. *PRINT THE LETTER OF THE CORRECT ANSWER IN THE SPACE AT THE RIGHT.*

1. Which of the following actions by a supervisor is LEAST likely to result in an increase in morale or productivity?   1.____

    A. Delegating additional responsibility but not authority to his subordinates
    B. Spending more time than his subordinates in planning and organizing the office's work
    C. Giving positive rather than negative orders to his subordinates
    D. Keeping his subordinates informed about changes in rules or policies which affect their work

Questions 2-8.

DIRECTIONS: Questions 2 through 8 are based SOLELY on the information and the form given below.

The following form is a Weekly Summary of New Employees and lists all employees appointed to Department F in the week indicated. In addition to the starting date and name, the form includes each new employee's time card number, title, status, work location and supervisor's name.

DEPARTMENT F

Weekly Summary of New Employees — Week Starting March 25

Starting Date	Name Last, First	Time Card No.	Title	Status	Work Location	Supervisor
3/25	Astaire, Hannah	361	Typist	Prov.	Rm. 312	Merrill, Judy
3/25	Silber, Arthur	545	Clerk	Perm.	Rm. 532	Rizzo, Joe
3/26	Vecchio, Robert	620	Accountant	Perm.	Rm. 620	Harper, Ruth
3/26	Goldberg, Sally	373	Stenographer	Prov.	Rm. 308	Merrill, Judy
3/26	Yee, Bruce	555	Accountant	Perm.	Rm. 530	Rizzo, Joe
3/27	Dunning, Betty	469	Typist	Perm.	Rm. 411	Miller, Tony
3/28	Goldman, Sara	576	Stenographer	Prov.	Rm. 532	Rizzo, Joe
3/29	Vesquez, Roy	624	Accountant	Perm.	Rm. 622	Harper, Ruth
3/29	Browning, David	464	Typist	Perm.	Rm. 411	Miller, Tony

50

2. On which one of the following dates did two employees *in the same title* begin work? 2.____

   A. 3/25   B. 3/26   C. 3/27   D. 3/29

3. To which one of the following supervisors was ONE typist assigned? 3.____

   A. Judy Merrill   B. Tony Miller
   C. Ruth Harper   D. Joe Rizzo

4. Which one of the following supervisors was assigned the GREATEST number of new employees during the week of March 25? 4.____

   A. Ruth Harper   B. Judy Merrill
   C. Tony Miller   D. Joe Rizzo

5. Which one of the following employees was assigned *three days after another employee* to the same job location? 5.____

   A. Sara Goldman   B. David Browning
   C. Bruce Yee   D. Roy Vesquez

6. The title in which BOTH provisional and permanent appointments were made is 6.____

   A. accountant   B. clerk   C. stenographer   D. typist

7. The employee who started work on the SAME day and have the SAME status but DIFFERENT titles are 7.____

   A. Arthur Silber and Hannah Astaire
   B. Robert Vecchio and Bruce Yee
   C. Sally Goldberg and Sara Goldman
   D. Roy Vesquez and David Browning

8. On the basis of the information given on the form, which one of the following conclusions regarding time card numbers appears to be CORRECT? 8.____

   A. The first digit of the time card number is coded according to the assigned title.
   B. The middle digit of the time card number is coded according to the assigned title.
   C. The first digit of the time card number is coded according to the employees' floor locations.
   D. Time card numbers are randomly assigned.

9. Assume that a caller arrives at your desk and states that she is your supervisor's daughter and that she would like to see her father. You have been under the impression that your supervisor has only a two-year-old son.
   Of the following, the BEST way to deal with this visitor is to 9.____

   A. offer her a seat and advise your supervisor of the visitor
   B. tell her to go right in to her father's office
   C. ask her for some proof to show that she is your supervisor's daughter
   D. escort her into your supervisor's office and ask him if the visitor is his daughter

10. Assume that you answer the telephone and the caller says that he is a police officer and asks for personal information about one of your co-workers.
    Of the following, the BEST course of action for you to take is to 10.____

A. give the caller the information he has requested
B. ask the caller for the telephone number of the phone he is using, call him back, and then give him the information
C. refuse to give him any information and offer to transfer the call to your supervisor
D. ask the caller for his name and badge number before giving him the information

Questions 11-16.

DIRECTIONS: Questions 11 through 16 each consist of a sentence which may or may not be an example of good English usage. Consider grammar, punctuation, spelling, capitalization, awkwardness, etc. Examine each sentence, and then choose the correct statement about it from the four choices below it. If the English usage in the sentence given is better than it would be with any of the changes suggested in Options B, C, or D, choose Option A. Do not choose an option that will change the meaning of the sentence.

11. The recruiting officer said, "There are many different goverment jobs available."

    A. This is an example of acceptable writing.
    B. The word *There* should not be capitalized.
    C. The word *goverment* should be spelled *government*.
    D. The comma after the word *said* should be removed.

12. He can recommend a mechanic whose work is reliable.

    A. This is an example of acceptable writing.
    B. The word *reliable* should be spelled *relyable*.
    C. The word *whose* should be spelled *who's*.
    D. The word *mechanic* should be spelled *mecanic*.

13. She typed quickly; like someone who had not a moment to lose.

    A. This is an example of acceptable writing.
    B. The word *not* should be removed.
    C. The semicolon should be changed to a comma.
    D. The word *quickly* should be placed before instead of after the word *typed*.

14. She insisted that she had to much work to do.

    A. This is an example of acceptable writing.
    B. The word *insisted* should be spelled *incisted*.
    C. The word *to* used in front of *much* should be spelled *too*.
    D. The word *do* should be changed to *be done*.

15. He excepted praise from his supervisor for a job well done.

    A. This is an example of acceptable writing.
    B. The word *excepted* should be spelled *accepted*.
    C. The order of the words *well done* should be changed to *done well*.
    D. There should be a comma after the word *supervisor*

16. What appears to be intentional errors in grammar occur several times in the passage.

    A. This is an example of acceptable writing.
    B. The word *occur* should be spelled *occurr*.
    C. The word *appears* should be changed to *appear*.
    D. The phrase *several times* should be changed to *from time to time*.

17. The daily compensation to be paid to each consultant hired in a certain agency is computed by dividing his professional earnings in the previous year by 250. The maximum daily compensation they can receive is $200 each. Four consultants who were hired to work on a special project had the following professional earnings in the previous year: $37,500, $44,000, $46,500, and $61,100.
    What will be the TOTAL DAILY COST to the agency for these four consultants?

    A. $932   B. $824   C. $756   D. $712

18. In a typing and stenographic pool consisting of 30 employees, 2/5 of them are typists, 1/3 of them are senior typists and senior stenographers, and the rest are stenographers. If there are 5 more stenographers than senior stenographers, how many senior stenographers are in the typing and stenographic pool?

    A. 3   B. 5   C. 8   D. 10

19. There are 3330 copies of a three-page report to be collated. One clerk starts collating at 9:00 A.M. and is joined 15 minutes later by two other clerks. It takes 15 minutes for each of these clerks to collate 90 copies of the report.
    At what time should the job be completed if ALL three clerks continue working at the SAME rate without breaks?

    A. 12:00 Noon   B. 12:15 P.M.   C. 1:00 P.M.   D. 1:15 P.M.

20. By the end of last year, membership in the blood credit program in a certain agency had increased from the year before by 500, bringing the total to 2500.
    If the membership increased by the same percentage this year, the TOTAL number of members in the blood credit program for this agency by the end of this year should be

    A. 2625   B. 3000   C. 3125   D. 3250

21. During this year, an agency suggestion program put into practice suggestions from 24 employees, thereby saving the agency 40 times the amount of money it paid in awards. If 1/3 of the employees were awarded $50 each, 1/2 of the employees were awarded $25 each, and the rest were awarded $10 each, how much money did the agency SAVE by using the suggestions?

    A. $18,760   B. $29,600   C. $32,400   D. $46,740

22. Which of the following actions should a supervisor generally find MOST effective as a method of determining whether subordinates need additional training in performing their work?

    A. Compiling a list of absences and latenesses of subordinates
    B. Observing the manner in which his subordinates carry out their various tasks
    C. Reviewing the grievances submitted by subordinates
    D. Reminding his subordinates to consult him if they experience difficulty in completing an assignment

23. Of the following types of letters, the MOST difficult to trace if lost after mailing is the _____ letter.

    A. special delivery
    B. registered
    C. insured
    D. certified

24. Suppose that you are looking over a few incoming letters that have been put in your mail basket. You see that one has a return address on the envelope but not on the letter itself. Of the following, the BEST way to make sure there is a correct record of the return address is to

    A. return the letter to the sender and ask him to fill in his address on his own letter
    B. put the letter back into the envelope and close the opening with a paper clip
    C. copy the address onto a 3"x5" index card and throw away the envelope
    D. copy the address onto the letter and staple the envelope to the letter

25. Although most incoming mail that you receive in an office will pertain to business matters, there are times when a letter may be delivered for your supervisor that is marked *Personal*.
    Of the following, the BEST way for you to handle this type of mail is to

    A. open the letter but do not read it, and route it along with the other mail
    B. read the letter to see if it really is personal
    C. have the letter forwarded unopened to your supervisor's home address
    D. deliver the letter to your supervisor's desk unopened

KEY (CORRECT ANSWERS)

1.	A	11.	C
2.	B	12.	A
3.	A	13.	C
4.	D	14.	C
5.	A	15.	B
6.	D	16.	C
7.	D	17.	D
8.	C	18.	A
9.	A	19.	B
10.	C	20.	C

21. B
22. B
23. D
24. D
25. D

EXAMINATION SECTION
TEST 1

DIRECTIONS: Each question or incomplete statement is followed by several suggested answers or completions. Select the one that BEST answers the question or completes the statement. *PRINT THE LETTER OF THE CORRECT ANSWER IN THE SPACE AT THE RIGHT.*

1. As the newly appointed supervisor of a unit in a city agency, you are about to design a system for measuring the quantity of work produced by your subordinates.
   The one of the following which is the FIRST step that you should take in designing this system is to

   A. establish the units of work measurement to be used in the system
   B. determine the actual advantages and disadvantages of the system
   C. determine the abilities of each of your subordinates
   D. ascertain the types of work done in the unit

   1.____

2. Suppose that you are the supervisor of a small unit in a city agency. One of your subordinates tells you that he is dissatisfied with his work assignment and that he wishes to discuss the matter with you. The employee is obviously very angry and upset.
   Of the following, the course of action that you should take FIRST in this situation is to

   A. postpone discussion of the employee's complaint, explaining to him that the matter can be settled more satisfactorily if it is discussed calmly
   B. have the employee describe his complaint, correcting him whenever he makes what seems to be an erroneous charge against you
   C. permit the employee to present his complaint in full, withholding your comments until he has finished describing his complaint
   D. promise the employee that you will review all the work assignments in the unit to determine whether or not any changes should be made

   2.____

3. Assume that you are the supervisor of a unit in a city agency. One of your subordinates has violated an important rule of the agency. For such a violation, you are required to impose discipline in the form of a reprimand given in private.
   Of the following, the MOST important reason for disciplining the employee for violating the rule is to

   A. obtain his compliance with the rule
   B. punish him for his action in an impartial manner
   C. establish your authority to administer discipline
   D. impress upon all the employees in the unit the need for observing the rule

   3.____

4. Miss Green is assigned to type weekly reports to be submitted to her supervisor, Mr. Brown. Before she begins working on the reports, he tells her that they should be neat in appearance. The first two reports she submits are unsatisfactory to Mr. Brown because they contain a few erasures, and he tells her that they are unsatisfactory. The next two reports she submits are unsatisfactory because they contain many erasures. Mr. Brown accepts these two reports without criticizing them. The fifth report she submits contains fewer erasures than the previous reports but it, too, is unsatisfactory because of its erasures. In order to prevent the submission of unsatisfactory reports in the future, Mr. Brown criticizes the erasures in her fifth report. She seems puzzled and upset by his criticism.
Mr. Brown's handling of Miss Green was faulty CHIEFLY because

   A. he did not give her sufficient opportunity to correct the work herself
   B. she may not have been capable of doing neat work
   C. he was inconsistent in his criticism of her work
   D. he should have criticized the reports containing many erasures rather than the reports with only a few erasures

5. You are the newly-appointed supervisor of a small unit in a city agency. One of your subordinates, Mr. Smith, a competent employee, has resented your appointment as his supervisor and has not been as cooperative toward you as you have wanted him to be. One day, Mr. Smith fails to observe an important rule of the agency. You are required to reprimand any employee who fails to observe the rule.
The one of the following courses of action you should take in this situation is to

   A. attempt to overcome Mr. Smith's resentment by explaining to him that although you should reprimand him, you will not do so
   B. reprimand Mr. Smith after pointing out to him that he failed to observe the rule
   C. tell Mr. Smith that if he becomes more cooperative, you will overlook his failure to observe the rule
   D. tell Mr. Smith that although you did not originate the rule, nevertheless you are required to reprimand him

6. Suppose that a clerk who has injured himself on the job because of his carelessness informs his supervisor of the accident. The supervisor has been newly appointed to his job and is anxious to keep accidents at a minimum. The action taken by the supervisor is to critize the subordinate for his carelessness and to tell him that he is holding him responsible for the accident.
Of the following, it would be MOST reasonable to conclude that, as a result of the supervisor's action, his subordinates may

   A. tend to withhold information from him about future accidents
   B. be critical of him, in turn, if he himself is injured on the job
   C. expect him to supervise them more closely in the future
   D. attempt to correct hazardous job conditions without his knowledge

7. The one of the following which is generally the BASIC reason for using standard procedures in an agency is to

   A. provide sequences of steps for handling recurring activities
   B. facilitate periodic review of standard practices

C. train new employees in the agency's policies and objectives
D. serve as a basis for formulating agency policies

8. Assume that the operations of a certain unit in a public agency enable the supervisor to allow each of his subordinates wide discretion in selecting the kind and amount of work he chooses to do. However, in evaluating the work of his subordinates, the supervisor places more emphasis on some areas of their work than on others. Factors such as number of applications processed and number of letters written are given great weight in evaluation, while factors such as number of papers filed and number of forms checked are given little weight. Hence, a subordinate who processes a large number of applications would receive a high evaluation even if he checked very few forms.
The supervisor's method of evaluation would MOST likely result in a(n)

   A. increase in the amount of time spent on processing each application
   B. backlog of papers waiting to be filed
   C. improvement in the quality of letters written
   D. decline in output in all areas of work

9. Some management authorities propose that work assignments be made by assigning a varied set of tasks to a group of employees and then allowing the group to decide for itself how to organize the work to be done. This method of assigning work is called *job enlargement*.
The one of the following which is considered to be the CHIEF advantage of job enlargement is that it

   A. encourages employees to specialize in the work they are assigned to do
   B. reduces the amount of control that employees have over their work
   C. increases the employees' job satisfaction
   D. reduces the number of skills that each employee is required to learn

10. In conducting a meeting to pass along information to his subordinates, a supervisor may talk to his subordinates without giving them the opportunity to interrupt him. This method is called one-way communication. On the other hand, the supervisor may talk to his subordinates and give them the opportunity to ask questions or make comments while he is speaking. This method is called two-way communication.
It would be more desirable for the supervisor to use two-way communication rather than one-way communication at a meeting when his primary purpose is to

   A. avoid, during the meeting, open criticism of any mistakes he may make
   B. conduct the meeting in an orderly fashion
   C. pass along information quickly
   D. transmit information which must be clearly understood

11. Assume that you are the leader of a training conference on supervisory techniques and problems. One of the participants in the conference proposes what you consider to be an unsatisfactory technique for handling the problem under discussion.
The one of the following courses of action which you should take in this situation is to

   A. explain to the participants why the proposed technique is unsatisfactory
   B. stimulate the other participants to discuss the appropriateness of the proposed technique

C. proceed immediately to another problem without discussing the proposed technique
D. end further discussion of the problem but explain to the participant in private, after the conference is over, why his proposed technique is unsatisfactory

12. In measuring the work of his subordinates, the supervisor of a unit performing routine filing began by observing his subordinates at work. If a subordinate seemed to be busy, then the supervisor concluded that the subordinate was producing a great deal of work. On the other hand, the supervisor concluded that a subordinate was not producing much work if he did not seem to be busy.
The supervisor's work measurement method was faulty CHIEFLY because

A. it did not use a standard against which a subordinate's work could be measured
B. the type of work performed by his subordinates did not lend itself to accurate measurement
C. his subordinates may not have worked at their normal rates if they were aware that their work was being observed
D. the supervisor may not have observed a subordinate's work for a long enough period of time

13. Assume that a system of statistical reports designed to provide information about employee work performance is put into effect in a unit of a city agency. There is some evidence that the employees of this unit are working below their capacities. The information obtained from the system is to be used by management to improve employee work and performance and to evaluate such performance. The employees whose work is to be recorded by the reports resent them. Nevertheless, the employees' work performance improves substantially after the reporting system is put into effect and before management has put the information to use.
The one of the following which is the MOST accurate conclusion to be drawn from this situation is that

A. a statistical reporting system may fail to provide the information it is designed to provide
B. low employee morale may have been the cause of the employees' former level of work performance
C. a statistical reporting system designed only to provide information about problems may also help to solve the problems
D. willing employee cooperation is essential to the success of a system of statistical reports

14. In setting the work standard for a certain task, a unit supervisor took the total output of all the employees in the unit and divided it by the number of employees. He thus established the average output as the work standard for the task.
The method that the supervisor used to establish the work standard is GENERALLY considered to be

A. *proper,* since the method takes into account the output of the outstanding, as well as of the less productive, employees.
B. *improper,* since the average output may not be what could reasonably be expected of a competent, satisfactory employee

C. *proper,* since the standard is based on the actual output of the employees who are to be evaluated
D. *improper,* since all the employees in the unit may be successful in meeting the work standard

15. There are disadvantages as well as advantages in using statistical controls to measure specific aspects of subordinates' jobs.
The one of the following which can LEAST be considered to be an advantage of statistical controls to a supervisor is that such controls may

    A. reduce the need for close, detailed supervision
    B. give the supervisor information that he needs for making decisions
    C. stimulate subordinates whose work is measured by statistical controls to improve their performance
    D. encourage subordinates to emphasize aspects being measured rather than their jobs as a whole

Questions 16-17.

DIRECTIONS: Questions 16 and 17 are to be answered SOLELY on the basis of the information contained below.

In public agencies, the success of a person assigned to perform first-line supervisory duties depends in large part upon the personal relations between him and his subordinate employees. The goal of supervising effort is something more than to obtain compliance with procedures established by some central office. The major objective is work accomplishment. In order for this goal to be attained, employees must want to attain it and must exercise initiative in their work. Only if employees are generally satisfied with the type of supervision which exists in an organization will they put forth their best efforts.

16. According to the above paragraph, in order for employees to try to do their work as well as they can, it is essential that

    A. they participate in determining their working conditions and rates of pay
    B. their supervisors support the employees' viewpoints in meetings with higher management
    C. they are content with the supervisory practices which are being used
    D. their supervisors make the changes in work procedures that the employees request

17. It can be inferred from the above paragraph that the goals of a unit in a public agency will NOT be reached unless the employees in the unit

    A. wish to reach them and are given the opportunity to make individual contributions to the work
    B. understand the relationship between the goals of the unit and the goals of the agency
    C. have satisfactory personal relationships with employees of other units in the agency
    D. carefully follow the directions issued by higher authorities

Questions 18-20.

DIRECTIONS: Questions 18 through 20 are to be answered SOLELY on the basis of the information below.

Discontent of some citizens with the practices and policies of local government leads here and there to creation of those American institutions, the local civic associations. Completely outside of government, manned by a few devoted volunteers, understaffed, and with pitifully few dues-paying members, they attempt to arouse widespread public opinion on selected issues by presenting facts and ideas. The findings of these civic associations are widely trusted by press and public, and amidst the records of rebuffs received are found more than enough achievements to justify what little their activities cost. Civic associations can, by use of initiative, get constructive measures placed on the ballot and the influence of these associations is substantial when brought to bear on a referendum question. Civic associations are politically non-partisan. Hence, their vitality is drawn from true political independents, who in most communities are a trifling minority. Except in a few large cities, civic associations are seldom affluent enough to maintain an office or to afford even a small paid staff.

18. It can be inferred from the above paragraph that the MAIN reason for the formation of civic associations is to

   A. provide independent candidates for local public office with an opportunity to be heard
   B. bring about changes in the activities of local government
   C. allow persons who are politically non-partisan to express themselves on local public issues
   D. permit the small minority of true political independents to supply leadership for non-partisan causes

19. According to the above paragraph, the statements which civic associations make on issues of general interest are

   A. accepted by large segments of the public
   B. taken at face value only by the few people who are true political independents
   C. questioned as to their accuracy by most newspapers
   D. expressed as a result of aroused widespread public opinion

20. On the basis of the information concerning civic associations contained in the above paragraph, it is MOST accurate to conclude that since

   A. they deal with many public issues, the cost of their efforts on each issue is small
   B. their attempts to attain their objectives often fail, little money is contributed to civic associations
   C. they spend little money in their efforts, they are ineffective when they become involved in major issues
   D. their achievements outweigh the small cost of their efforts, civic associations are considered worthwhile

7 (#1)

21. Assume that, in an office of a city agency, correspondence is filed, according to the date received, in 12 folders, one for each month of the year. On January 1 of each year, correspondence dated through December 31 of the preceding year is transferred from the active to the inactive files. New folders are then inserted in the active files to contain the correspondence to be filed in the next year.
The one of the following which is the CHIEF disadvantage of this method of transferring correspondence from active to inactive files is that

    A. the inactive files may lack the capacity to contain all the correspondence transferred to them
    B. the folders prepared each year must be labeled the same as the folders in preceding years
    C. some of the correspondence from the preceding year may not be in the active files on January 1
    D. some of the correspondence transferred to the inactive files may be referred to as frequently as some of the correspondence in the active files

21.____

22. A clerk who is assigned to inspect office equipment in a large number of offices in a city agency is given a checklist of defects to look for in the equipment in each office.
Of the following, the CHIEF advantage of the checklist is that

    A. the number of defects for which the clerk must look is kept to a minimum
    B. the defects listed on the checklist will not be overlooked
    C. the defects listed on the checklist may suggest to the clerk other defects for which he might look
    D. each defect listed on the checklist will be checked only once

22.____

23. If 50,000 copies of a form are to be reproduced, the one of the following types of duplicating machines that would be the MOST suitable is the

    A. mimeograph   B. photocopy
    C. offset   D. digital duplicator

23.____

24. Of the following, the MAIN reason for keeping a perpetual inventory of supplies in a storeroom is that such an inventory

    A. provides a continuous record of supplies on hand
    B. eliminates the need for a physical inventory
    C. indicates which supplies are in greatest demand
    D. encourages economy in the use of supplies

24.____

25. Assume that you are the head of a unit in a city agency. From time to time, your subordinates are assigned to other units to do reception work and other duties. You receive a note from Mr. Jones, the head of one of these other units, stating that the work of Miss Smith, one of your subordinates, was unsatisfactory when she worked for him, and asking you not to assign her to him again. Although Miss Smith has worked in your unit for a long time, this is the first time that anyone has complained about her work.
The one of the following actions that you should take FIRST in this situation is to ask

    A. the heads of the other units for whom Miss Smith has worked whether or not her work has been satisfactory
    B. Mr. Jones in what way Miss Smith's work has been unsatisfactory

25.____

61

C. Miss Smith to explain in what way her work for Mr. Jones was unsatisfactory
D. Mr. Jones which of your subordinates he would prefer to have assigned to him

26. Suppose that you are the supervisor of a small unit in a city agency. You have given one of your subordinates, Mr. Smith, an assignment which must be completed by the end of the day. Because he is unfamiliar with the assignment, Mr. Smith will be unable to complete it on time. Your other subordinates are too busy to help Mr. Smith, but you have the time to help him complete the assignment. For you to help Mr. Smith complete the assignment would be

   A. *desirable,* because a supervisor is expected to be familiar with his subordinates' work
   B. *undesirable,* because Mr. Smith will come to depend on you to help him do his work
   C. *desirable,* because Mr. Smith is likely to appreciate your help and give you his cooperation when you need it
   D. *undesirable,* because a supervisor should not perform the same type of work as his subordinates do

27. For a supervisor to listen to the personal problems which his subordinates bring to him is GENERALLY

   A. *desirable;* it is likely that the supervisor has broader experience in solving personal problems than do his subordinates
   B. *undesirable;* the supervisor may be unable to solve such problems
   C. *desirable;* the supervisor can better understand his subordinates' behavior on the job
   D. *undesirable;* permitting a subordinate to talk about his personal problems may only make them seem worse

28. A generally accepted concept of management is that the authority given to a person should be commensurate with his

   A. responsibility   B. ability
   C. seniority   D. dependability

29. *It has been said that the best supervisor is the one who gives the fewest orders.*
    The one of the following supervisory practices that would be MOST likely to increase the number of orders that a supervisor must give to get out the work is to

   A. set general goals for his subordinates and give them the authority for reaching the goals
   B. train subordinates to make decisions for themselves
   C. establish routines for his subordinates' jobs
   D. introduce frequent changes in the work methods his subordinates are using

30. The one of the following supervisory practices that would be MOST likely to give subordinates in a unit of a public agency a feeling of satisfaction in their work is to

    A. establish work goals that take a long time to achieve
    B. show the subordinates how their work goals are related to the goals of the agency
    C. set work goals higher than the subordinates can achieve
    D. refrain from telling the subordinates that they are failing to meet their work goals

30.____

KEY (CORRECT ANSWERS)

1.	D	16.	C
2.	C	17.	A
3.	A	18.	B
4.	C	19.	A
5.	B	20.	D
6.	A	21.	D
7.	A	22.	B
8.	B	23.	C
9.	C	24.	A
10.	D	25.	B
11.	B	26.	C
12.	A	27.	C
13.	C	28.	A
14.	B	29.	D
15.	D	30.	B

TEST 2

DIRECTIONS: Each question or incomplete statement is followed by several suggested answers or completions. Select the one that BEST answers the question or completes the statement. *PRINT THE LETTER OF THE CORRECT ANSWER IN THE SPACE AT THE RIGHT.*

Questions 1-5.

DIRECTIONS: Each of Questions 1 through 5 consists of a statement which contains one word that is incorrectly used because it is not in keeping with the meaning that the statement is evidently intended to convey. Determine which word is INCORRECTLY used. Then, select from among the words lettered A, B, C, or D the word which, when substituted for the incorrectly used word, would BEST help to convey the meaning of the statement. Indicate in the space at the right the letter preceding the word you have selected.

1. It is hard to determine whether the large or small organization would receive the greater benefit from scientific work measurement, for while the large organization undoubtedly receives greater returns in terms of money savings, the effect of proportionate savings on a small organization is probably ever more incertain.

   A. beneficial B. certainly
   C. unimportant D. precise

2. Under a good personnel policy, the number of employee complaints and grievances will tend to be a number which is sufficiently great to keep the supervisory force on its toes and yet large enough to leave time for other phases of supervision.

   A. limit B. definite C. complete D. small

3. If the supervisor of a group of employees is to supply the necessary leadership to his subordinates, they will seek a leader outside the group for guidance, assistance, and inspiration, because leadership must be supplied by someone whenever human beings work together for a common objective.

   A. plan B. produce
   C. information D. fails

4. Organization and management techniques that facilitate delegation of work should be taught to supervisors, thus enabling them to maintain control while participating in the details of every operation.

   A. without B. coordination
   C. instructing D. simplify

5. In whatever form and at whatever intervals, the written report submitted by the operating unit can never adequately supplement personal, firsthand acquaintance with the work.

   A. comprehensive B. objective
   C. replace D. experience

64

Questions 6-23.

DIRECTIONS: Each of Questions 6 through 23 consists of a word in capitals followed by four suggested meanings of the word. For each question, indicate in the space at the right the letter preceding the word which means MOST NEARLY the same as the word in capitals.

6. AMENABLE
    A. lukewarm   B. responsive
    C. binding   D. durable

7. CONDUCIVE
    A. respectful   B. combined
    C. helpful   D. confusing

8. EXTOL
    A. praise   B. explain
    C. remind   D. extend

9. TRANSITION
    A. peace   B. brief period
    C. change   D. final action

10. PARITY
    A. participation   B. equality
    C. payment   D. bias

11. SUBTERFUGE
    A. substitute   B. strong bias
    C. confirmation   D. deception

12. PERVASIVE
    A. dishonest   B. penetrating
    C. contrary   D. eager

13. RECAPITULATE
    A. surrender   B. reply
    C. summarize   D. restrict

14. TRANSCEND
    A. surpass   B. interpret
    C. remove   D. transfer

15. MITIGATE
    A. prevent   B. take for granted
    C. argue   D. make milder

16. RETROSPECT
    A. proof   B. review of the past
    C. reluctance   D. clear judgment

17. PERMEATE
    A. make a lasting impression   B. exert pressure
    C. spread through   D. take into account

18. CRITERION

    A. accomplishment   B. standard
    C. challenge   D. improvement

19. PERPETRATE

    A. commit   B. continue indefinitely
    C. conceal   D. unable to solve

20. INSUPERABLE

    A. inappropriate   B. weighty
    C. unconquerable   D. responsible

21. CULMINATE

    A. amass rapidly   B. concentrate on
    C. search for   D. reach the highest point

22. VARIANCE

    A. disadvantage   B. choice
    C. fault   D. difference

23. PERNICIOUS

    A. harmful   B. anxious
    C. deliberate   D. insolent

Questions 24-31.

DIRECTIONS: Each of Questions 24 through 31 consists of two sentences. Either or both of these sentences may contain errors in grammar, sentence structure, punctuation, or spelling, or both sentences may be correct. Consider a sentence correct if it contains no errors, although there may be other correct ways of writing the sentence. Indicate your answer in the space at the right as follows:
Indicate the letter
    A if only sentence I contains an error;
    B if only sentence II contains an error;
    C if both sentences I and II contain errors;
    D if both sentences are correct.

24. I. No employee considered to be indispensable will be assigned to the new office.
    II. The arrangement of the desks and chairs give the office a neat appearance.

25. I. The recommendation, accompanied by a report, was delivered this morning.
    II. Mr. Green thought the procedure would facilitate his work; he knows better now.

26. I. A dictionary, in addition to the office management textbooks, were placed on his desk.
    II. The concensus of opinion is that none of the employees should be required to work overtime.

27. I. Mr. Granger has demonstrated that he is as courageous, if not more courageous, then Mr. Brown.
    II. The successful completion of the project depends on the manager's accepting our advisory opinion.

27._____

28. I. Mr. Ames was in favor of issuing a set of rules and regulations for all of us employees to follow.
    II. It is inconceivable that the new clerk knows how to deal with that kind of correspondence.

28._____

29. I. The revised referrence manual is to be used by all of the employees.
    II. Mr. Johnson told Miss Kent and me to accumulate all the letters that we receive.

29._____

30. I. The supervisor said, that before any changes would be made in the attendance report, there must be ample justification for them.
    II. Each of them was asked to amend their preliminary report.

30._____

31. I. Mrs. Peters conferred with Mr. Roberts before she laid the papers on his desk.
    II. As far as this report is concerned, Mr. Williams always has and will be responsible for its preparation.

31._____

Questions 32-39.

DIRECTIONS: Questions 32 through 39 are to be answered SOLELY on the basis of the information contained in the chart and table shown below which relate to Bureau X in a certain public agency. The chart shows the percentage of the bureau's annual expenditures spent on equipment, supplies, and salaries for each of the years 2011-2015. The table shows the bureau's annual expenditures for each of the years 2011-2015. Equipment, supplies, and salaries were the only three categories for which the bureau spent money.

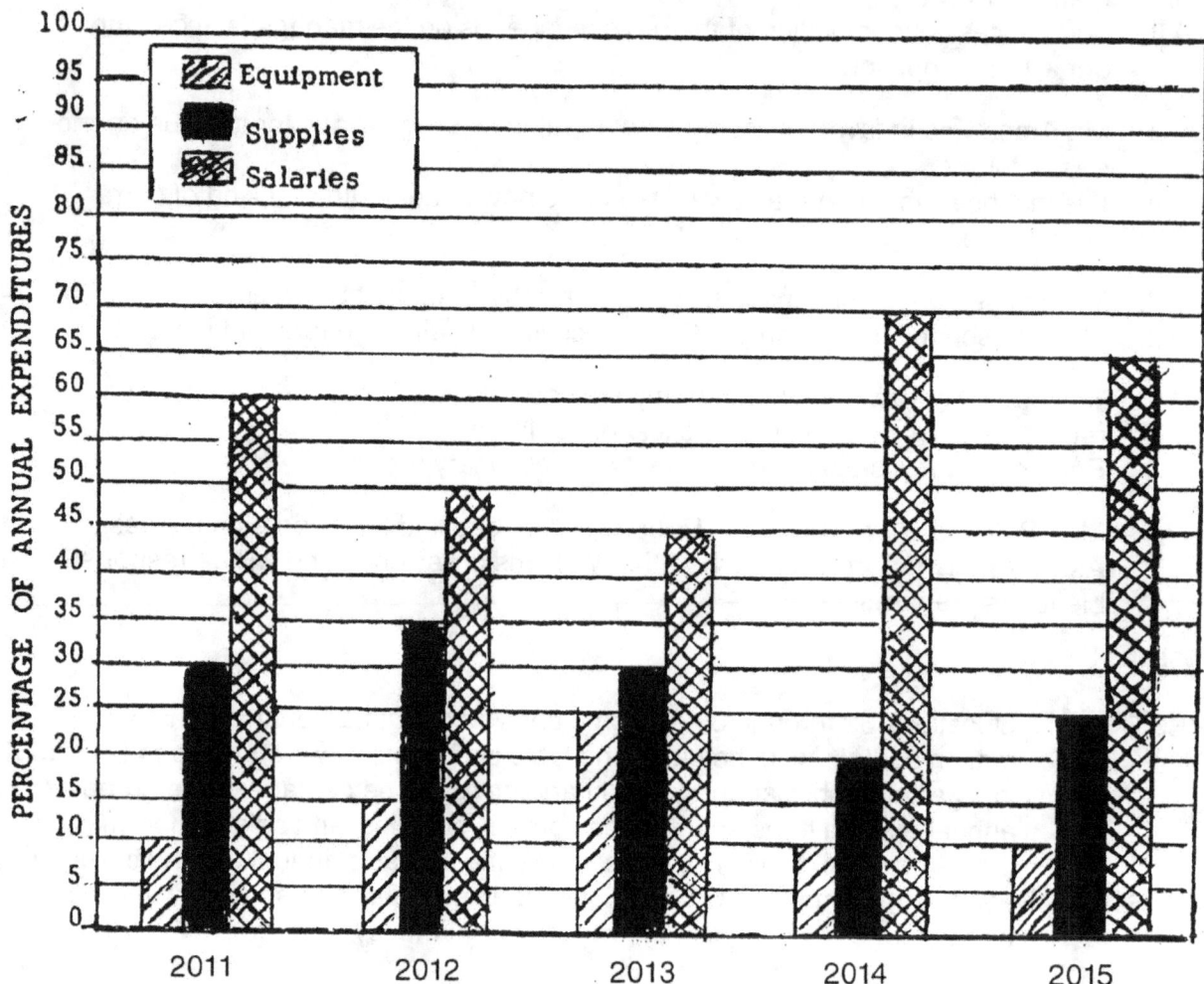

The bureau's annual expenditures for the years 2011-2015 are shown in the following table:

YEAR	EXPENDITURES
2011	$ 8,000,000
2012	12,000,000
2013	15,000,000
2014	10,000,000
2015	12,000,000

The information contained in the chart and table is sufficient to determine the   32.____

A. average annual salary of an employee in the bureau in 2012
B. decrease in the amount of money spent on supplies in the bureau in 2011 from the amount spent in the preceding year
C. changes, between 2013 and 2014, in the prices of supplies bought by the bureau
D. increase in the amount of money spent on salaries in the bureau in 2015 over the amount spent in the preceding year

33. If the percentage of expenditures for salaries in one year is added to the percentage of expenditures for equipment in that year, a total of two percentages for that year is obtained.
The two years for which this total is the SAME are

    A. 2011 and 2013
    B. 2012 and 2014
    C. 2011 and 2014
    D. 2012 and 2015

33.____

34. Of the following, the year in which the bureau spent the GREATEST amount of money on supplies was

    A. 2015   B. 2013   C. 2012   D. 2011

34.____

35. Of the following years, the one in which there was the GREATEST increase over the preceding year in the amount of money spent on salaries is

    A. 2014   B. 2015   C. 2012   D. 2013

35.____

36. Of the bureau's expenditures for equipment in 2015, one-third was used for the purchase of mailroom equipment and the remainder was spent on miscellaneous office equipment. How much did the bureau spend on miscellaneous office equipment in 2015?

    A. $4,000,000
    B. $400,000
    C. $8,000,000
    D. $800,000

36.____

37. If there were 120 employees in the bureau in 2014, then the average annual salary paid to the employees in that year was MOST NEARLY

    A. $43,450   B. $49,600   C. $58,350   D. $80,800

37.____

38. In 2013, the bureau had 125 employees.
If 20 of the employees earned an average annual salary of $80,000, then the average salary of the other 105 employees was MOST NEARLY

    A. $49,000   B. $64,000   C. $41,000   D. $54,000

38.____

39. Assume that the bureau estimated that the amount of money it would spend on supplies in 2016 would be the same as the amount it spent on that category in 2015. Similarly, the bureau estimated that the amount of money it would spend on equipment in 2016 would be the same as the amount it spent on that category in 2015. However, the bureau estimated that in 2016 the amount it would spend on salaries would be 10 percent higher than the amount it spent on that category in 2015.
The percentage of its annual expenditures that the bureau estimated it would spend on supplies in 2016 is MOST NEARLY

    A. 27.5%   B. 23.5%   C. 22.5%   D. 25%

39.____

40. Each side of a square room which is being used as an office measures 66 feet. The floor of the room is divided by six traffic aisles, each aisle being six feet wide. Three of the aisles run parallel to the east and west sides of the room, and the other three run parallel to the north and south sides of the room, so that the remaining floor space is divided into 16 equal sections. If all of the floor space which is not being used for traffic aisles is occupied by desk and chair sets, and each set takes up 24 square feet of floor space, the number of desk and chair sets in the room is

    A. 80   B. 64   C. 36   D. 96

40.____

KEY (CORRECT ANSWERS)

1.	A	11.	D	21.	D	31.	B
2.	D	12.	B	22.	D	32.	D
3.	D	13.	C	23.	A	33.	A
4.	A	14.	A	24.	B	34.	B
5.	C	15.	D	25.	D	35.	C
6.	B	16.	B	26.	C	36.	D
7.	C	17.	C	27.	A	37.	C
8.	A	18.	B	28.	B	38.	A
9.	C	19.	A	29.	A	39.	B
10.	B	20.	C	30.	C	40.	D

EXAMINATION SECTION
TEST 1

DIRECTIONS: Each question or incomplete statement is followed by several suggested answers or completions. Select the one that BEST answers the question or completes the statement. *PRINT THE LETTER OF THE CORRECT ANSWER IN THE SPACE AT THE RIGHT.*

Questions 1-4.

DIRECTIONS: Questions 1 through 4 are to be answered SOLELY on the basis of the following passage.

Job analysis combined with performance appraisal is an excellent method of determining training needs of individuals. The steps in this method are to determine the specific duties of the job, to evaluate the adequacy with which the employee performs each of these duties, and finally to determine what significant improvements can be made by training.

The list of duties can be obtained in a number of ways: asking the employee, asking the supervisor, observing the employee, etc. Adequacy of performance can be estimated by the employee, but the supervisor's evaluation must also be obtained. This evaluation will usually be based on observation.

What does the supervisor observe? The employee, while he is working; the employee's work relationships; the ease, speed, and sureness of the employee's actions; the way he applies himself to the job; the accuracy and amount of completed work; its conformity with established procedures and standards; the appearance of the work; the soundness of judgment it shows; and, finally, signs of good or poor communication, understanding, and cooperation among employees.

Such observation is a normal and inseparable part of the everyday job of supervision. Systematically, recorded, evaluated, and summarized, it highlights both general and individual training needs.

1. According to the passage, job analysis may be used by the supervisor in   1.____
    A. increasing his own understanding of tasks performed in his unit
    B. increasing efficiency of communication within the organization
    C. assisting personnel experts in the classification of positions
    D. determining in which areas an employee needs more instruction

2. According to the passage, the FIRST step in determining the training needs of   2.____
   employees is to
    A. locate the significant improvements that can be made by training
    B. determine the specific duties required in a job
    C. evaluate the employee's performance
    D. motivate the employee to want to improve himself

3. On the basis of the above passage, which of the following is the BEST way for a supervisor to determine the adequacy of employee performance?
   A. Check the accuracy and amount of completed work
   B. Ask the training officer
   C. Observe all aspects of the employee's work
   D. Obtain the employee's own estimate

4. Which of the following is NOT mentioned by the passage as a factor to be taken into consideration in judging the adequacy of employee performance?
   A. Accuracy of completed work
   B. Appearance of completed work
   C. Cooperation among employees
   D. Attitude of the employee toward his supervisor

5. In indexing names of business firms and other organizations, ONE of the rules to be followed is:
   A. The word *and* is considered an indexing unit.
   B. When a firm name includes the full name of a person who is not well-known, the person's first name is considered as the first indexing unit.
   C. Usually the units in a firm name are indexed in the order in which they are written.
   D. When a firm's name is made up of single letters (such as ABC Corp.), the letters taken together are considered more than one indexing unit.

6. Assume that people often come to your office with complaints of errors in your agency's handling of their clients. The employees in your office have the job of listening to these complaints and investigating them. One day, when it is almost closing time, a person comes into your office, apparently very angry, and demands that you take care of his complaint at once.
   Your IMMEDIATE reaction should be to
   A. suggest that he return the following day
   B. find out his name and the nature of his complaint
   C. tell him to write a letter
   D. call over your supervisor

7. Assume that part of your job is to notify people concerning whether their applications for a certain program have been approved or disapproved. However, you do not actually make the decision on approval or disapproval. One day, you answer a telephone call from a woman who states that she has not yet received any word on her application. She goes on to tell you her qualifications for the program. From what she has said, you know that persons with such qualifications are usually approved.
   Of the following, which one is the BEST thing for you to say to her?
   A. "You probably will be accepted, but wait until you receive a letter before trying to join the program."
   B. "Since you seem well qualified, I am sure that your application will be approved."

C. "If you can write us a letter emphasizing your qualifications, it may speed up the process."
D. "You will be notified of the results of your application as soon as a decision has been made."

8. Suppose that one of your duties includes answering specific telephone inquiries. Your superior refers a call to you from an irate person who claims that your agency is inefficient and is wasting taxpayers' money.
Of the following, the BEST way to handle such a call is to
   A. listen briefly and then hang up without answering
   B. note the caller's comments and tell him that you will transmit them to your superiors
   C. connect the caller with the head of your agency
   D. discuss your own opinions with the caller

8.____

9. An employee has been assigned to open her division head's mail and place it on his desk. One day, the employee opens a letter which she then notices is marked *Personal*.
Of the following, the BEST action for her to take is to
   A. write *Personal* on the letter and staple the envelope to the back of the letter
   B. ignore the matter and treat the letter the same way as the others
   C. give it to another division head to hold until her own division head comes into the office
   D. leave the letter in the envelope and write *Sorry opened by mistake* on the envelope and initial it

9.____

Questions 10-14.

DIRECTIONS: Questions 10 through 14 each consist of a quotation which contains one word that is incorrectly used because it is not in keeping with the meaning that the quotation is evidently intended to convey. Of the words underlined in each quotation, determine which word is incorrectly used. Then select from among the words lettered A, B, C, and D the word which, when substituted for the incorrectly used word, would BEST help to convey the meaning of the quotation. (Do not indicate a change for an underlined word unless the underlined word is incorrectly used.)

10. Unless reasonable managerial supervision is <u>exercised</u> over office supplies, it is certain that there will be extravagance, <u>rejected</u> items out of stock, <u>excessive</u> prices paid for certain items, and <u>obsolete</u> material in the stockroom.
   A. overlooked   B. immoderate   C. needed   D. instituted

10.____

11. Since <u>office</u> supplies are in such <u>common</u> use, an attitude of indifference about their handling is not <u>unusual</u>. Their importance is often recognized only when they are <u>utilized</u> or out of stock, for office employees must have proper supplies if maximum productivity is to be <u>attained</u>.
   A. plentiful   B. unavailable   C. reduced   D. expected

11.____

12. Anyone <u>effected</u> by paperwork, <u>interested</u> in or engaged in office work, or desiring to improve <u>informational</u> activities can find materials <u>keyed</u> to his needs.
    A. attentive   B. available   C. affected   D. ambitious

13. Information is <u>homogeneous</u> and must therefore be properly classified so that each type may be <u>employed</u> in ways <u>appropriate</u> to its <u>own peculiar</u> properties.
    A. apparent
    B. heterogeneous
    C. consistent
    D. idiosyncratic

14. <u>Intellectual</u> training may seem a <u>formidable</u> phrase, but it means nothing more than the <u>deliberate</u> cultivation of the ability to think, and there is no <u>dark</u> contrast between the intellectual and the practical.
    A. subjective   B. objective   C. sharp   D. vocational

15. The MOST important reason for having a filing system is to
    A. get papers out of the way
    B. have a record of everything that has happened
    C. retain information to justify your actions
    D. enable rapid retrieval of information

16. The system of filing which is used MOST frequently is called _____ filing.
    A. alphabetic
    B. alphanumeric
    C. geographic
    D. numeric

17. One of the clerks under your supervision has been telephoning frequently to tell you that he was taking the day off. Unless there is a real need for it, taking leave which is not scheduled is frowned upon because it upsets the work schedule.
    Under these circumstances, which of the following reasons for taking the day off is MOST acceptable?
    A. "I can't work when my arthritis bothers me."
    B. "I've been pressured with work from my night job and needed the extra time to catch up."
    C. "My family just moved to a new house, and I needed the time to start the repairs."
    D. "Work here has not been challenging, and I've been looking for another job."

18. One of the employees under your supervision, previously a very satisfactory worker, has begun arriving late one or two mornings each week. No explanation has been offered for this change. You call her to your office for a conference. As you are explaining the purpose of the conference and your need to understand this sudden lateness problem, she becomes very angry and states that you have no right to question her.
    Of the following, the BEST course of action for you to take at this point is to

A. inform her in your most authoritarian tone that you are the supervisor and that you have every right to question her
B. end the conference and advise the employee that you will have no further discussion with her until she controls her temper
C. remain calm, try to calm her down, and when she has quieted, explain the reasons for your questions and the need for answers
D. hold your temper; when she has calmed down, tell her that you will not have a tardy worker in your unit and will have her transferred at once

19. Assume that, in the branch of the agency for which you work, you are the only clerical person on the staff with a supervisory title and, in addition, that you are the office manager. On a particular day when all members of the professional staff are away from the building attending an important meeting, an urgent call comes through requesting some confidential information ordinarily released only by professional staff.
Of the following, the MOST reasonable action for you to take is to
    A. decline to give the information because you are not a member of the professional staff
    B. offer to call back after you get permission from the agency director at the main office
    C. advise the caller that you will supply the information as soon as your chief returns
    D. supply the information requested and inform your chief when she returns

20. As a supervisor, you are scheduled to attend an important conference with your superior. However, that day you learn that your very capable assistant is ill and unable to come to work. Several highly sensitive tasks are scheduled for completion on this day.
Of the following, the BEST way to handle this situation is to
    A. tell your supervisor you cannot attend the meeting and ask that it be postponed
    B. assign one of your staff to see that the jobs are completed and turned in
    C. advise your supervisor of the situation and ask what you should do
    D. call the departments for which the work is being done and ask for an extension of time

21. When a decision needs to be made which is likely to affect units other than his own, a supervisor should USUALLY
    A. make such a decision quickly and then discuss it with his supervisor
    B. make such a decision only after careful consultation with his subordinates
    C. discuss the problem with his immediate superior before making such a decision
    D. have his subordinates arrive at such a decision in conference with the subordinates in the other units

22. Assume that, as a supervisor in Division X, you are training Ms. Y, a new employee, to answer the telephone properly.
You should explain that the BEST way to answer is to pick up the receiver and say:

A. "What is your name, please?"   B. "May I help you?"
C. "Ms. Y speaking."   D. "Division X, Ms. Y speaking."

Questions 23-25.

DIRECTIONS: Questions 23 through 25 consist of sentences in which two words are missing. Examine each sentence, and then choose from below it the words which should be inserted in the blank spaces in order to create a coherent and well-written sentence.

23. Human behavior is far _____ variable, and therefore _____ predictable, than that of any other species.   23.____
    A. less; as   B. less; not   C. more; not   D. more; less

24. The _____ limitation of this method is that the results are based _____ a narrow sample.   24.____
    A. chief; with   B. chief; on   C. only; for   D. only; to

25. Although there _____ a standard procedure for handling these problems, each case often has _____ own unique features.   25.____
    A. are; its   B. are; their   C. is; its   D. is; their

KEY (CORRECT ANSWERS)

1.	D		11.	B
2.	B		12.	C
3.	C		13.	B
4.	D		14.	C
5.	C		15.	D
6.	B		16.	A
7.	D		17.	A
8.	B		18.	C
9.	D		19.	B
10.	C		20.	C

21. C
22. D
23. D
24. B
25. C

TEST 2

DIRECTIONS: Each question or incomplete statement is followed by several suggested answers or completions. Select the one that BEST answers the question or completes the statement. *PRINT THE LETTER OF THE CORRECT ANSWER IN THE SPACE AT THE RIGHT.*

Questions 1-3.

DIRECTIONS: Questions 1 through 3 each consist of a group of four sentences. Read each sentence carefully, and select the one of the four in each group which represents the BEST English usage for business letters and reports.

1. A. The chairman himself, rather than his aides, has reviewed the report.
    B. The chairman himself, rather than his aides, have reviewed the report.
    C. The chairmen, not the aide, has reviewed the report.
    D. The aide, not the chairmen, have reviewed the report.

2. A. Various proposals were submitted but the decision is not been made.
    B. Various proposals has been submitted but the decision has not been made.
    C. Various proposals were submitted but the decision is not been made.
    D. Various proposals have been submitted but the decision has not been made.

3. A. Everyone were rewarded for his successful attempt.
    B. They were successful in their attempts and each of them was rewarded.
    C. Each of them are rewarded for their successful attempts.
    D. The reward for their successful attempts were made to each of them.

4. Which of the following is MOST suited to arrangement in chronological order?
    A. Applications for various types and levels of jobs
    B. Issues of a weekly publication
    C. Weekly time cards for all employees for the week of April 21
    D. Personnel records for all employees

5. Words that are *synonymous* with a given word ALWAYS _____ the given word.
    A. have the same meaning as   B. have the same pronunciation as
    C. have the opposite meaning of D. can be rhymed with

Questions 6-11.

DIRECTIONS: Questions 6 through 11 are to be answered on the basis of the following chart showing numbers of errors made by four clerks in one work unit for a half-year period.

77

	Allan	Barry	Cary	David
July	5	4	1	7
August	8	3	9	8
September	7	8	7	5
October	3	6	5	3
November	2	4	4	6
December	5	2	8	4

6. The clerk with the HIGHEST number of errors for the six-month period was
   A. Allan   B. Barry   C. Cary   D. David

   6.____

7. If the number of errors made by Allan in the six months shown represented one-eighth of the total errors made by the unit during the entire year, what was the TOTAL number of errors made by the unit for the year?
   A. 124   B. 180   C. 240   D. 360

   7.____

8. The number of errors made by David in November was what FRACTION of the total errors made in November?
   A. 1/3   B. 1/6   C. 3/8   D. 3/16

   8.____

9. The average number of errors made per month per clerk was MOST NEARLY
   A. 4   B. 5   C. 6   D. 7

   9.____

10. Of the total number of errors made during the six-month period, the percentage made in August was MOST NEARLY
    A. 2%   B. 4%   C. 23%   D. 4%

    10.____

11. If the number of errors in the unit were to decrease in the next six months by 30%, what would be MOST NEARLY the total number of errors for the unit for the next six months?
    A. 87   B. 94   C. 120   D. 137

    11.____

12. The arithmetic mean salary for five employees earning $18,500, $18,300, $18,600, $18,400, and $18,500, respectively is
    A. $18,450   B. $18,460   C. $18,475   D. $18,500

    12.____

13. Last year, a city department which is responsible for purchasing supplies ordered bond paper in equal quantities from 22 different companies. The price was exactly the same for each company, and the total cost for the 22 orders was $693,113.
    Assuming prices did not change during the year, the cost of EACH order was MOST NEARLY
    A. $31,490   B. $31,495   C. $31,500   D. $31,505

    13.____

14. A city agency engaged in repair work uses a small part which the city purchases for $0.14 each. Assume that, in a certain year, the total expenditure of the city for this part was $700.
How MANY of these parts were purchased that year?
A. 50 B. 200 C. 2,000 D. 5,000

15. The work unit which you supervise is responsible for processing fifteen reports per month.
If your unit has four clerks and the best worker completes 40% of the reports himself, how many reports would each of the other clerks have to complete if they all do an equal number?
A. 1 B. 2 C. 3 D. 4

16. Assume that the work unit in which you work has 24 clerks and 18 stenographers. In order to change the ratio of stenographers to clerks so that there is one stenographer for every four clerks, it would be necessary to REDUCE the number of stenographers by
A. 3 B. 6 C. 9 D. 12

17. Assume that your office is responsible for opening and distributing all the mail of the division. After opening a letter, one of your subordinates notices that it states that there should be an enclosure in the envelope. However, there is no enclosure in the envelope.
Of the following, the BEST instruction that you can give the clerk is to
A. call the sender to obtain the enclosure
B. call the addressee to inform him that the enclosure is missing
C. note the omission in the margin of the letter
D. forward the letter without taking any action

18. While opening the envelope containing official correspondence, you accidentally cut the enclosed letter.
Of the following, the BEST action for you to take is to
A. leave the material as it is
B. put it together by using transparent mending tape
C. keep it together by putting it back in the envelope
D. keep it together by using paper clips

19. Suppose your supervisor is on the telephone in his office and an applicant arrives for a scheduled interview with him.
Of the following, the BEST procedure to follow ordinarily is to
A. informally chat with the applicant in your office until your supervisor has finished his phone conversation
B. escort him directly into your supervisor's office and have him wait for him there
C. inform your supervisor of the applicant's arrival and try to make the applicant feel comfortable while waiting
D. have him hang up his coat and tell him to go directly in to see your supervisor

20. The length of time that files should be kept is GENERALLY
    A. considered to be seven years
    B. dependent upon how much new material has accumulated in the files
    C. directly proportionate to the number of years the office has been in operation
    D. dependent upon the type and nature of the material in the files

21. Cross-referencing a document when you file it means
    A. making a copy of the document and putting the copy into a related file
    B. indicating on the front of the document the name of the person who wrote it, the date it was written, and for what purpose
    C. putting a special sheet or card in a related file to indicate where the document is filed
    D. indicating on the document where it is to be filed

22. Unnecessary handling and recording of incoming mail could be eliminated by
    A. having the person who opens it initial it
    B. indicating on the piece of mail the names of all the individuals who should see it
    C. sending all incoming mail to more than one central location
    D. making a photocopy of each piece of incoming mail

23. Of the following, the office tasks which lend themselves MOST readily to planning and study are
    A. repetitive, occur in volume, and extend over a period of time
    B. cyclical in nature, have small volume, and extend over a short period of time
    C. tasks which occur only once in a great while not according to any schedule, and have large volume
    D. special tasks which occur only once, regardless of their volume and length of time

24. A good recordkeeping system includes all of the following procedures EXCEPT the
    A. filing of useless records
    B. destruction of certain files
    C. transferring of records from one type of file to another
    D. creation of inactive files

25. Assume that, as a supervisor, you are responsible for orienting and training new employees in your unit.
    Which of the following can MOST properly be omitted from your discussions with a new employee?
    A. The purpose of commonly used office forms
    B. Time and leave regulations
    C. Procedures for required handling of routine business calls
    D. The reason the last employee was fired

KEY (CORRECT ANSWERS)

1.	A	11.	A
2.	D	12.	B
3.	B	13.	D
4.	B	14.	D
5.	A	15.	C
6.	C	16.	D
7.	C	17.	C
8.	C	18.	B
9.	B	19.	C
10.	C	20.	D

21. C
22. B
23. A
24. A
25. D

EXAMINATION SECTION
TEST 1

DIRECTIONS: Each question or incomplete statement is followed by several suggested answers or completions. Select the one that BEST answers the question or completes the statement. *PRINT THE LETTER OF THE CORRECT ANSWER IN THE SPACE AT THE RIGHT.*

1. The _____ on the data processing staff is responsible for determining if a new application should be developed.   1._____

    A. programmer
    B. analyst
    C. operator
    D. database administrator
    E. all of the above

2. A collection of files grouped together so that data may be independently retrieved from each file is a   2._____

    A. file
    B. record
    C. database
    D. file management system
    E. data bank

3. The data processing cycle consists of input,   3._____

    A. processing, output
    B. arithmetic, logic, output
    C. storage, output
    D. processing, storage, output
    E. arithmetic, logic, storage, output

4. Before any data may be processed, it MUST reside   4._____

    A. on tape
    B. on video cards
    C. in computer memory
    D. on the video screen
    E. on the printer

5. _____ may be stored on magnetic disk.   5._____

    A. Characters
    B. Fields
    C. Records
    D. Databases
    E. All of the above

6. An example of a source document is a   6._____

    A. bill produced by a computer
    B. a graph generated by a spreadsheet program
    C. handwritten list of items to be entered into a computer
    D. checking statement sent by a bank to a customer
    E. all of the above

7. Data integrity refers to _____ entry of data into the computer system.   7._____

    A. accurate
    B. reliable
    C. timely
    D. all of the above
    E. none of the above

8. The process of arranging a list of names in alphabetical order is called

   A. indexing   B. sorting   C. reporting
   D. searching   E. selection

9. The MAIN components of a computerized report are

   A. heading, detail lines, summary
   B. data entry screen, editing area, data validation area
   C. heading, control breaks, summary
   D. heading, subtotal lines, summary
   E. heading and summary lines

10. _____ terminals are computer terminals which also have processing capabilities.

    A. Keyboard   B. Dumb
    C. Remote job entry D. Intelligent
    E. Stand-alone

11. The process of transferring data over a communication line from a mainframe computer to a microcomputer is

    A. uploading   B. downloading
    C. modem transmission D. electronic mail
    E. networking

12. During _____, data is entered onto storage media, then re-entered again to ensure the accuracy of the data.

    A. editing   B. validation checking
    C. bi-keying   D. key verification
    E. double verification

13. A(n) _____ printer is an example of a high-speed printer.

    A. ink jet   B. laser   C. thermal
    D. photo   E. all of the above

14. A(n) _____ report is NOT produced by a computer.

    A. detail   B. exception   C. projection
    D. summary   E. all of the above

15. A _____ video screen displays only one color.

    A. VGA   B. color   C. monochrome
    D. CRT   E. all of the above

16. The _____ printer is BEST suited to print graphic output.

    A. dot matrix B. ink jet   C. plotter
    D. chain   E. thermal

17. Which of the following can be used for entering data into a computer?

    A. OCR   B. Mouse   C. Keyboard
    D. Light pen E. All of the above

18. Database management systems use a special class of commands in order that a user may facilitate extracting data from the database.
    This class of commands is called _____ language.

    A. query by example B. query
    C. inquiry D. programming
    E. procedure

19. An acceptable response time from when the user requests data from the computer to the time the user receives a response is under _____ seconds.

    A. 60   B. 30   C. 15   D. 10   E. 3

20. The part of computer memory which may be accessed by the user for storage and retrieving his own data is called

    A. RAM   B. ROM   C. EPROM   D. PROM   E. DROM

21. The part of the CPU which directs the sequence of instructions and flow of data is the

    A. ALU B. control unit C. memory
    D. logic unit E. arithmetic unit

22. _____ is the placement on disk or tape of two or more consecutive records in between interblock gaps.

    A. Gapping B. Blocking C. Staggering
    D. Sequencing E. Sorting

23. When updating a sequential file,

    A. *only* the record being updated is changed
    B. *only* the record and those preceding it are changed
    C. the entire file must be read and rewritten
    D. *only* the record being updated and those following it are changed
    E. two new files are created

24. Sequential files are used PRIMARILY for

    A. backup data B. on-line processing
    C. interactive processing D. timesharing
    E. all of the above

25. In a hierarchial database, data is stored in a _____ relationship.

    A. father-son B. member-owner C. sequential
    D. direct E. none of the above

KEY (CORRECT ANSWERS)

1. B
2. C
3. D
4. C
5. E

6. C
7. D
8. B
9. A
10. D

11. B
12. D
13. E
14. C
15. C

16. C
17. E
18. B
19. E
20. A

21. B
22. B
23. C
24. A
25. B

TEST 2

DIRECTIONS: Each question or incomplete statement is followed by several suggested answers or completions. Select the one that BEST answers the question or completes the statement. *PRINT THE LETTER OF THE CORRECT ANSWER IN THE SPACE AT THE RIGHT.*

1. The _____ communication line allows the short distance (50-75 miles) transmission of data through the airwaves. 1.____

    A. satellite B. fiber-optics C. laser
    D. microwave E. coaxial

2. _____ data transmission permits *only* one character to be transmitted at a time. 2.____

    A. Full duplex B. Half duplex C. Asynchronous
    D. Parallel E. Simplex

3. During _____, the computer *asks* a terminal if it has data to process. 3.____

    A. polling B. surveying C. inquiry
    D. dialing E. calling

4. _____ is a centralized type of computer network used on larger computer systems. 4.____

    A. LAN B. Star network
    C. Ring network D. Distributed network
    E. All of the above

5. An advantage of low-level languages over high-level languages is that low-level languages 5.____

    A. are easier to write in
    B. are easier to find and correct errors
    C. can make optimum use of computer resources
    D. need very few instructions to write a complete program
    E. all of the above are advantages

6. The software to be loaded FIRST before any other software can be loaded into the computer is the 6.____

    A. applications program B. utility programs
    C. operating system D. compilers
    E. programming languages

7. Which of the following is NOT an operating system? 7.____

    A. OS/VS B. MS-DOS C. UNIX
    D. OS2 E. Cobol

8. A _____ graphically describes the flow of data through a system. 8.____

    A. data flow diagram B. hierarchy chart
    C. pseudocode D. HIPO chart
    E. Gantt chart

9. A list of the files, records, fields, etc. used in a system is maintained in a

   A. program maintenance notebook
   B. data dictionary
   C. system documentation manual
   D. operator's manual
   E. transaction log

10. A(n) _____ is generated by a computerized business system to track accounting transactions back to their source.

    A. transaction log
    B. data dictionary
    C. audit trail
    D. system flowchart
    E. all of the above

11. A _____ is used to schedule the time it will take to complete computer tasks or program development.

    A. system flowchart
    B. data flow diagram
    C. Gantt chart
    D. data dictionary
    E. transaction log

12. Which conversion method is used for converting a manual system to a computerized system?

    A. Parallel
    B. Direct
    C. Test-site
    D. All of the above
    E. None of the above

13. The organization responsible for the standardization of programming languages and procedures is

    A. NCAA   B. ANSI   C. NCAP   D. CODASYL   E. DLL

14. The process whereby a program is reviewed step by step in an effort to uncover flaws in the program is called

    A. flowcharting
    B. pseudocode
    C. structured walkthrough
    D. IPO
    E. data flow diagramming

15. Which of the following is an application for personal computers?

    A. Word processing
    B. Electronic spreadsheets
    C. Database management systems
    D. Computerized accounting systems
    E. All of the above

16. Which of the following is an entry-level position?

    A. Analyst
    B. Applications programmer
    C. Systems programmer
    D. Database administrator
    E. Lead programmer

17. *Computer security* refers to protection from

   A. unauthorized users
   B. abusive users
   C. misuse of computer resources
   D. disasters such as fire and flood
   E. all of the above

18. The process of transforming a telephone (analog) to a computer (digital) signal so that it may be understood by the computer system is called

   A. modulation
   B. demodulation
   C. analogation
   D. digitalization
   E. multiplexing

19. The _____ computer numbering system uses both number and letter symbols to represent values.

   A. binary
   B. digital
   C. decimal
   D. octal
   E. hexadecimal

20. One type of computer file contains data that is relatively *static,* that is, data that does not change on a regular basis. This file is treated as an authority on records which are associated with it.
    This paragraph BEST describes a(n) _____ file.

   A. transaction
   B. index
   C. master
   D. memory
   E. authority

21. A _____ is a set of rules which governs the transmission of data over a communications channel.

   A. protocol
   B. handshake
   C. sequencer
   D. modem
   E. algorithm

22. This technique is used to transmit large quantities of data from the CPU to tape or disk so that it can be output through a low-speed device such as a printer. The CPU is then free to process other data.
    This paragraph BEST describes the process of

   A. modulation
   B. demodulation
   C. spooling
   D. updating
   E. transaction processing

23. One type of computer memory uses disk or tape to store portions of software not in use. With this type of memory, the computer has almost unlimited main memory capacity.
    This paragraph BEST describes

   A. VLSI
   B. VSAM
   C. virtual memory
   D. partioned memory
   E. dynamic memory

24. *Throughput* measures computer

   A. memory capacity
   B. storage capacity

4 (#2)

   C. speed at which work can be processed
   D. CPU speed
   E. all of the above

25. EBCDIC, ASCII, and Hollerith code are all   25.____
   A. hexadecimal codes
   B. binary codes
   C. zoned coding systems
   D. used on magnetic storage devices (disk and tape)
   E. used to represent numeric values only

KEY (CORRECT ANSWERS)

1.	D	11.	C
2.	C	12.	D
3.	A	13.	B
4.	B	14.	C
5.	C	15.	E
6.	C	16.	B
7.	E	17.	E
8.	A	18.	A
9.	B	19.	E
10.	C	20.	C

21. A
22. C
23. C
24. C
25. C

SPELLING

EXAMINATION SECTION

TEST 1

DIRECTIONS: Each question or incomplete statement is followed by several suggested answers or completions. Select the one that BEST answers the question or completes the statement. *PRINT THE LETTER OF THE CORRECT ANSWER IN THE SPACE AT THE RIGHT.*

Questions 1-5.

DIRECTIONS: Questions 1 through 5 consist of four words. Indicate the letter of the word that is CORRECTLY spelled.

1. A. harassment B. harrasment 1.____
   C. harasment D. harrassment

2. A. maintainance B. maintenence 2.____
   C. maintainence D. maintenance

3. A. comparable B. comprable 3.____
   C. comparible D. commparable

4. A. suficient B. sufficiant 4.____
   C. sufficient D. suficiant

5. A. fairly   B. fairley   C. farely   D. fairlie   5.____

Questions 6-10.

DIRECTIONS: Questions 6 through 10 consist of four words. Indicate the letter of the word that is INCORRECTLY spelled.

6. A. pallor   B. ballid   C. ballet   D. pallid   6.____

7. A. urbane B. surburbane 7.____
   C. interurban D. urban

8. A. facial   B. physical   C. fiscle   D. muscle   8.____

9. A. interceed B. benefited 9.____
   C. analogous D. altogether

10. A. seizure B. irrelevant 10.____
    C. inordinate D. dissapproved

KEY (CORRECT ANSWERS)

1. A 6. B
2. D 7. B
3. A 8. C
4. C 9. A
5. A 10. D

TEST 2

DIRECTIONS: Each of Questions 1 through 15 consists of two words preceded by the letters A and B. In each question, one of the words may be spelled INCORRECTLY or both words may be spelled CORRECTLY. If one of the words in a question is spelled INCORRECTLY, print in the space at the right the capital letter preceding the INCORRECTLY spelled word. If both words are spelled CORRECTLY, print the letter C.

1. A. easely   B. readily   1.____
2. A. pursue   B. decend   2.____
3. A. measure   B. laboratory   3.____
4. A. exausted   B. traffic   4.____
5. A. discussion   B. unpleasant   5.____
6. A. campaign   B. murmer   6.____
7. A. guarantee   B. sanatary   7.____
8. A. communication   B. safty   8.____
9. A. numerus   B. celebration   9.____
10. A. nourish   B. begining   10.____
11. A. courious   B. witness   11.____
12. A. undoubtedly   B. thoroughly   12.____
13. A. accessible   B. artifical   13.____
14. A. feild   B. arranged   14.____
15. A. admittence   B. hastily   15.____

KEY (CORRECT ANSWERS)

1.	A	6.	B	11.	A
2.	B	7.	B	12.	C
3.	C	8.	B	13.	B
4.	A	9.	A	14.	A
5.	C	10.	B	15.	A

TEST 3

DIRECTIONS: In each of the following sentences, one word is misspelled. Following each sentence is a list of four words taken from the sentence. Indicate the letter of the word which is MISSPELLED in the sentence. *PRINT THE LETTER OF THE CORRECT ANSWER IN THE SPACE AT THE RIGHT.*

1. The placing of any inflammable substance in any building, or the placing of any device or contrivance capable of producing fire, for the purpose of causing a fire is an attempt to burn.
   A. inflammable
   B. substance
   C. device
   D. contrivence

2. The word *break* also means obtaining an entrance into a building by any artifice used for that purpose, or by collussion with any person therein.
   A. obtaining
   B. entrance
   C. artifice
   D. colussion

3. Any person who with intent to provoke a breech of the peace causes a disturbance or is offensive to others may be deemed to have committed disorderly conduct.
   A. breech
   B. disturbance
   C. offensive
   D. committed

4. When the offender inflicts a grevious harm upon the person from whose possession, or in whose presence, property is taken, he is guilty of robbery.
   A. offender
   B. grevious
   C. possession
   D. presence

5. A person who wilfuly encourages or advises another person in attempting to take the latter's life is guilty of a felony.
   A. wilfuly
   B. encourages
   C. advises
   D. attempting

6. He maliciously demurred to an ajournment of the proceedings.
   A. maliciously
   B. demurred
   C. ajournment
   D. proceedings

7. His innocence at that time is irrelevant in view of his more recent villianous demeanor.
   A. innocence
   B. irrelevant
   C. villianous
   D. demeanor

8. The mischievous boys aggrevated the annoyance of their neighbor.
   A. mischievous
   B. aggrevated
   C. annoyance
   D. neighbor

2 (#3)

9. While his perseverence was commendable, his judgment was debatable.   9.____
   A. perseverence   B. commendable
   C. judgment   D. debatable

10. He was hoping the appeal would facilitate his aquittal.   10.____
    A. hoping   B. appeal
    C. facilitate   D. aquittal

11. It would be preferable for them to persue separate courses.   11.____
    A. preferable   B. persue
    C. separate   D. courses

12. The litigant was complimented on his persistance and achievement.   12.____
    A. litigant   B. complimented
    C. persistance   D. achievement

13. Ocassionally there are discrepancies in the descriptions of miscellaneous items.   13.____
    A. ocassionally   B. discrepancies
    C. descriptions   D. miscellaneous

14. The councilmanic seargent-at-arms enforced the prohibition.   14.____
    A. councilmanic   B. seargeant-at-arms
    C. enforced   D. prohibition

15. The teacher had an ingenious device for maintaining attendance.   15.____
    A. ingenious   B. device
    C. maintaning   D. attendance

16. A worrysome situation has developed as a result of the assessment that absenteeism is increasing despite our conscientious efforts.   16.____
    A. worrysome   B. assessment
    C. absenteeism   D. conscientious

17. I concurred with the credit manager that it was practicable to charge purchases on a biennial basis, and the company agreed to adhear to this policy.   17.____
    A. concurred   B. practicable
    C. biennial   D. adhear

18. The pastor was chagrined and embarassed by the irreverent conduct of one of his parishioners.   18.____
    A. chagrined   B. embarassed
    C. irreverent   D. parishioners

19. His inate seriousness was belied by his flippant demeanor.   19.____
    A. inate   B. belied
    C. flippant   D. demeanor

20. It was exceedingly regrettable that the excessive number of challenges in the court delayed the start of the trial.
    A. exceedingly
    B. regrettable
    C. excessive
    D. challanges

20.____

KEY (CORRECT ANSWERS)

1.	D	11.	B
2.	D	12.	C
3.	A	13.	A
4.	B	14.	B
5.	A	15.	C
6.	C	16.	A
7.	C	17.	D
8.	B	18.	B
9.	A	19.	A
10.	D	20.	D

TEST 4

Questions 1-11.

DIRECTIONS: Each question consists of three words in each question, one of the words may be spelled incorrectly or all three may be spelled correctly. For each question if one of the words is spelled INCORRECTLY, write the letter of the incorrect word in the space at the right. If all three words are spelled CORRECTLY, write the letter D in the space at the right.

SAMPLE I: (A) guide   (B) departmint   (C) stranger
SAMPLE II: (A) comply   (B) valuable   (C) window
In Sample I, departmint is incorrect. It should be spelled department. Therefore, B is the answer.
In Sample II, all three words are spelled correctly. Therefore, D is the answer.

1. A. argument   B. reciept   C. complain   1._____
2. A. sufficient   B. postpone   C. visible   2._____
3. A. expirience   B. dissatisly   C. alternate   3._____
4. A. occurred   B. noticable   C. appendix   4._____
5. A. anxious   B. guarantee   C. calendar   5._____
6. A. sincerely   B. affectionately   C. truly   6._____
7. A. excellant   B. verify   C. important   7._____
8. A. error   B. quality   C. enviroment   8._____
9. A. exercise   B. advance   C. pressure   9._____
10. A. citizen   B. expence   C. memory   10._____
11. A. flexable   B. focus   C. forward   11._____

Questions 12-15.

DIRECTIONS: Each of Questions 12 through 15 consists of a group of four words. Examine each group carefully; then in the space at the right, indicate
A. if only one word in the group is spelled correctly
B. if two words in the group are spelled correctly
C. if three words in the group are spelled correctly
D. if all four words in the group are spelled correctly

12. Wendsday, particular, similar, hunderd   12._____

97

13. realize, judgment, opportunities, consistent   13.____

14. equel, principle, assistense, committee   14.____

15. simultaneous, privilege, advise, ocassionaly   15.____

KEY (CORRECT ANSWERS)

1.	B	6.	D	11.	A
2.	D	7.	A	12.	B
3.	A	8.	C	13.	D
4.	B	9.	D	14.	A
5.	C	10.	B	15.	C

TEST 5

DIRECTIONS: Each of Questions 1 through 15 consists of two words preceded by the letters A and B. In each item, one of the words may be spelled INCORRECTLY or both words may be spelled CORRECTLY. If one of the words in a question is spelled INCORRECTLY, print in the space at the right the letter preceding the INCORRECTLY spelled word. If bot words are spelled CORRECTLY, print the letter C.

1. A. justified   B. offering   1._____
2. A. predjudice   B. license   2._____
3. A. label   B. pamphlet   3._____
4. A. bulletin   B. physical   4._____
5. A. assure   B. exceed   5._____
6. A. advantagous   B. evident   6._____
7. A. benefit   B. occured   7._____
8. A. acquire   B. graditude   8._____
9. A. amenable   B. boundry   9._____
10. A. deceive   B. voluntary   10._____
11. A. imunity   B. conciliate   11._____
12. A. acknoledge   B. presume   12._____
13. A. substitute   B. prespiration   13._____
14. A. reputable   B. announce   14._____
15. A. luncheon   B. wretched   15._____

KEY (CORRECT ANSWERS)

1.	C	6.	A	11.	A
2.	A	7.	B	12.	A
3.	C	8.	B	13.	B
4.	C	9.	B	14.	A
5.	C	10.	C	15.	C

TEST 6

DIRECTIONS: Questions 1 through 15 contain lists of words, one of which is misspelled. Indicate the MISSPELLED word in each group. *PRINT THE LETTER OF THE CORRECT ANSWER IN THE SPACE AT THE RIGHT.*

1. A. felony B. lacerate 1.____
   C. cancellation D. seperate

2. A. batallion B. beneficial 2.____
   C. miscellaneous D. secretary

3. A. camouflage B. changeable 3.____
   C. embarrass D. inoculate

4. A. beneficial B. disasterous 4.____
   C. incredible D. miniature

5. A. auxilliary B. hypocrisy 5.____
   C. phlegm D. vengeance

6. A. aisle B. cemetary 6.____
   C. courtesy D. extraordinary

7. A. crystallize B. innoculate 7.____
   C. eminent D. symmetrical

8. A. judgment B. maintainance 8.____
   C. bouillon D. eery

9. A. isosceles B. ukulele 9.____
   C. mayonaise D. iridescent

10. A. remembrance B. occurence 10.____
    C. correspondence D. countenance

11. A. corpuscles B. mischievous 11.____
    C. batchelor D. bulletin

12. A. terrace B. banister 12.____
    C. concrete D. masonery

13. A. balluster B. gutter 13.____
    C. latch D. bridging

14. A. personnell B. navel 14.____
    C. therefor D. emigrant

100

15. A. committee B. submiting 15.____
    C. amendment D. electorate

KEY (CORRECT ANSWERS)

1.	D	6.	B	11.	C
2.	A	7.	B	12.	D
3.	C	8.	B	13.	A
4.	B	9.	C	14.	A
5.	A	10.	B	15.	B

TEST 7

Questions 1-5.

DIRECTIONS: Questions 1 through 5 consist of groups of four words. Select answer
A if only one word is spelled correctly in a group
B if TWO words are spelled correctly in a group
C if THREE words are spelled correctly in a group
D if all FOUR words are spelled correctly in a group.

1. counterfeit, embarass, panicky, supercede   1._____

2. benefited, personnel, questionnaire, unparalelled   2._____

3. bankruptcy, describable, proceed, vacuum   3._____

4. handicapped, mispell, offerred, pilgrimmage   4._____

5. corduroy, interfere, privilege, separator   5._____

Questions 6-10.

DIRECTIONS: Questions 6 through 10 consist of four pairs of words each. Some of the words are spelled correctly; others are spelled incorrectly. For each question, indicate in the space at the right the letter preceding that pair of words in which BOTH words are spelled CORRECTLY.

6. A. hygienic, inviegle   B. omniscience, pittance   6._____
   C. plagarize, nullify   D. seargent, perilous

7. A. auxilary, existence   B. pronounciation, accordance   7._____
   C. ignominy, indegence   D. suable, baccalaureate

8. A. discreet, inaudible   B. hypocrisy, currupt   8._____
   C. liquidate, maintainance   D. transparancy, onerous

9. A. facility; stimulent   B. frugel, sanitary   9._____
   C. monetary, prefatory   D. punctileous, credentials

10. A. bankruptsy, perceptible   B. disuade, resilient   10._____
    C. exhilerate, expectancy   D. panegyric, disparate

Questions 11-15.

DIRECTIONS: Each question or incomplete statement is followed by several suggested answers or completions. Select the one that BEST answers the question or completes the statement. PRINT THE LETTER OF THE CORRECT ANSWER IN THE SPACE AT THE RIGHT.

11. The silent *e* must be retained when the suffix *–able* is added to the word 11.____
    A. argue B. love C. move D. notice

12. The CORRECTLY spelled word in the choices below is 12.____
    A. kindergarden   B. zylophone
    C. hemorrhage   D. mayonaise

13. Of the following words, the one spelled CORRECTLY is 13.____
    A. begger   B. cemetary
    C. embarassed D. coyote

14.
    A. dandilion B. wiry C. sieze D. rythmic 14.____

15. A. beligerent   B. anihilation
    C. facetious   D. adversery

KEY (CORRECT ANSWERS)

1.	B	6.	B	11.	D
2.	C	7.	D	12.	C
3.	D	8.	A	13.	D
4.	A	9.	C	14.	B
5.	D	10.	D	15.	C

TEST 8

DIRECTIONS: In each of the following sentences, one word is misspelled. Following each sentence is a list of four words taken from the sentence. Indicate the letter of the word which is MISSPELLED. *PRINT THE LETTER OF THE CORRECT ANSWER IN THE SPACE AT THE RIGHT.*

1. If the administrator attempts to withold information, there is a good likelihood that there will be serious repercussions.
   A. administrator
   B. withold
   C. likelihood
   D. repercussions

   1._____

2. He condescended to apologize, but we felt that a beligerent person should not occupy an influential position.
   A. condescended
   B. apologize
   C. beligerent
   D. influential

   2._____

3. Despite the sporadic delinquent payments of his indebtedness, Mr. Johnson has been an exemplery customer.
   A. sporadic
   B. delinquent
   C. indebtedness
   D. exemplery

   3._____

4. He was appreciative of the support he consistantly acquired, but he felt that he had waited an inordinate length of time for it.
   A. appreciative
   B. consistantly
   C. acquired
   D. inordinate

   4._____

5. Undeniably they benefited from the establishment of a receivership, but the question of statutary limitations remained unresolved.
   A. undeniably
   B. benefited
   C. receivership
   D. statutary

   5._____

6. Mr. Smith profered his hand as an indication that he considered it a viable contract, but Mr. Nelson alluded to the fact that his colleagues had not been consulted.
   A. profered
   B. viable
   C. alluded
   D. colleagues

   6._____

7. The treatments were beneficial according to the optomotrists, and the consensus was that minimal improvement could be expected.
   A. beneficial
   B. optomotrists
   C. consensus
   D. minimal

   7._____

8. Her frivolous manner was unbecoming because the air of solemnity at the cemetery was pervasive.
   A. frivalous
   B. solemnity
   C. cemetery
   D. pervasive

   8._____

104

9. The clandestine meetings were designed to make the two adversaries more amicable, but they served only to intensify their emnity.
   A. clandestine
   B. adversaries
   C. amicable
   D. emnity

9.____

10. Do you think that his innovative ideas and financial acumen will help stabalize the fluctuations of the stock market?
    A. innovative
    B. acumen
    C. stabalize
    D. fluctuations

10.____

11. In order to keep a perpetual inventory, you will have to keep an uninterrupted surveillance of all the miscellanious stock.
    A. perpetual
    B. uninterrupted
    C. surveillance
    D. miscellanious

11.____

12. She used the art of pursuasion on the children because she found that caustic remarks had no perceptible effect on their behavior.
    A. pursuasion
    B. caustic
    C. perceptible
    D. effect

12.____

13. His sacreligious outbursts offended his constituents, and he was summarily removed from office by the City Council.
    A. sacreligious
    B. constituents
    C. summarily
    D. Council

13.____

14. They exhorted the contestants to greater efforts, but the exhorbitant costs in terms of energy expended resulted in a feeling of lethargy.
    A. exhorted
    B. contestants
    C. exhorbitant
    D. lethargy

14.____

15. Since he was knowledgable about illicit drugs, he was served with a subpoena to appear for the prosecution.
    A. knowledgable
    B. illicit
    C. subpoena
    D. prosecution

15.____

16. In spite of his lucid statements, they denigrated his report and decided it should be succintly paraphrased.
    A. lucid
    B. denigrated
    C. succintly
    D. paraphrased

16.____

17. The discussion was not germane to the contraversy, but the indicted man's insistence on further talk was allowed.
    A. germane
    B. contraversy
    C. indicted
    D. insistence

17.____

18. The legislators were enervated by the distances they had traveled during the election year to fullfil their speaking engagements.
    A. legislators
    B. enervated
    C. traveled
    D. fullfil

18.____

19. The plaintiffs' attornies charge the defendant in the case with felonious assault.
    A. plaintiffs'
    B. attornies
    C. defendant
    D. felonious

    19._____

20. It is symptomatic of the times that we try to placate all, but a proposal for new forms of disciplinery action was promulgated by the staff.
    A. symptomatic
    B. placate
    C. disciplinery
    D. promulgated

    20._____

KEY (CORRECT ANSWERS)

1.	B	11.	D
2.	C	12.	A
3.	D	13.	A
4.	B	14.	C
5.	D	15.	A
6.	A	16.	C
7.	B	17.	B
8.	A	18.	D
9.	D	19.	B
10.	C	20.	C

TEST 9

DIRECTIONS: Each of Questions 1 through 15 consists of a single word which is spelled either correctly or incorrectly. If the word is spelled CORRECTLY, you are to print the letter C (Correct) in the space at the right. If the word is spelled INCORRECTL, you are to print the letter W (Wrong).

1. pospone   1.____
2. diffrent   2.____
3. height   3.____
4. carefully 4.____
5. ability   5.____
6. temper   6.____
7. deslike   7.____
8. seldem   8.____
9. alcohol   9.____
10. expense   10.____
11. vegatable 11.____
12. dispensary 12.____
13. specemin 13.____
14. allowance 14.____
15. exersise 15.____

KEY (CORRECT ANSWERS)

1. W	6. C	11. W
2. W	7. W	12. C
3. C	8. W	13. W
4. C	9. C	14. C
5. C	10. C	15. W

TEST 10

DIRECTIONS: Each of Questions 1 through 10 consists of four words, one of which may be spelled incorrectly or all four words may be spelled correctly. If one of the words in a question is spelled incorrectly, print in the space at the right the capital letter preceding the word which is spelled INCORRECTLY. If all four words are spelled CORRECTLY, print the letter E.

1. A. dismissal B. collateral
   C. leisure D. proffession   1.____

2. A. subsidary B. outrageous
   C. liaison D. assessed   2.____

3. A. already B. changeable
   C. mischevous D. cylinder   3.____

4. A. supersede B. deceit
   C. dissension D. imminent   4.____

5. A. arguing B. contagious
   C. comparitive D. accessible   5.____

6. A. indelible B. existance
   C. presumptuous D. mileage   6.____

7. A. extention B. aggregate
   C. sustenance D. gratuitous   7.____

8. A. interrogate B. exaggeration
   C. vacillate D. moreover   8.____

9. A. parallel B. derogatory
   C. admissible D. appellate   9.____

10. A. safety B. cumalative
    C. disappear D. usable   10.____

KEY (CORRECT ANSWERS)

1.	D	6.	B
2.	A	7.	A
3.	C	8.	E
4.	E	9.	C
5.	C	10.	B

TEST 11

DIRECTIONS: Each of questions 1 through 10 consists of four words, one of which may be spelled incorrectly or all four words may be spelled correctly. If one of the words in a question is spelled INCORRECTLY, print in the space at the right the capital letter preceding the word which is spelled incorrectly. If all four words are spelled CORRECTLY, print the letter E.

1. A. vehicular   B. gesticulate   1._____
   C. manageable   D. fullfil

2. A. inovation   B. onerous   2._____
   C. chastise   D. irresistible

3. A. familiarize B. dissolution   3._____
   C. oscillate   D. superflous

4. A. census   B. defender   4._____
   C. adherence   D. inconceivable

5. A. voluminous   B. liberalize   5._____
   C. bankrupcy   D. conversion

6. A. justifiable B. executor   6._____
   C. perpatrate   D. dispelled

7. A. boycott   B. abeyence   7._____
   C. enterprise   D. circular

8. A. spontaineous B. dubious   8._____
   C. analyze   D. premonition

9. A. intelligible B. apparently   9._____
   C. genuine   D. crucial

10. A. plentiful   B. ascertain   10._____
    C. carreer   D. preliminary

KEY (CORRECT ANSWERS)

1. D   6. C
2. A   7. B
3. D   8. A
4. E   9. E
5. C   10. C

TEST 12

DIRECTIONS: Each of questions 1 through 25 consists of four words, one of which may be spelled incorrectly or all four words may be spelled correctly. If one of the words in a question is spelled INCORRECTLY, print in the space at the right the capital letter preceding the word which is spelled incorrectly. If all four words are spelled CORRECTLY, print the letter E.

1. A. temporary B. existance 1.____
   C. complimentary D. altogether

2. A. privilege B. changeable 2.____
   C. jeopardize D. commitment

3. A. grievous B. alloted 3.____
   C. outrageous D. mortgage

4. A. tempermental B. accommodating 4.____
   C. bookkeeping D. panicky

5. A. auxiliary B. indispensable 5.____
   C. ecstasy D. fiery

6. A. dissappear B. buoyant 6.____
   C. imminent D. parallel

7. A. loosly B. medicine 7.____
   C. schedule D. defendant

8. A. endeavor B. persuade 8.____
   C. retroactive D. desparate

9. A. usage B. servicable 9.____
   C. disadvantageous D. remittance

10. A. beneficary B. receipt 10.____
    C. excitable D. implement

11. A. accompanying B. intangible 11.____
    C. offerred D. movable

12. A. controlling B. seize 12.____
    C. repetitious D. miscellaneous

13. A. installation B. accommodation 13.____
    C. consistant D. illuminate

14. A. incidentaly B. privilege 14.____
    C. apparent D. chargeable

2 (#12)

15. A. prevalent B. serial 15.____
    C. briefly D. disatisfied

16. A. reciprocal B. concurrence 16.____
    C. persistence D. withold

17. A. deferred B. suing 17.____
    C. fulfilled D. pursuant

18. A. questionable B. omission 18.____
    C. acknowledgment D. insistent

19. A. guarantee B. committment 19.____
    C. mitigate D. publicly

20. A. prerogative B. apprise 20.____
    C. extrordinary D. continual

21. A. arrogant B. handicapped 21.____
    C. judicious D. perennial

22. A. permissable B. deceive 22.____
    C. innumerable D. retrieve

23. A. notable B. allegiance 23.____
    C. reimburse D. illegal

24. A. wholly B. disbursement 24.____
    C. hindrance D. conciliatory

25. A. guidance B. condemn 25.____
    C. publically D. coercion

KEY (CORRECT ANSWERS)

1.	B		11.	C
2.	E		12.	E
3.	B		13.	C
4.	A		14.	A
5.	E		15.	D
6.	A		16.	D
7.	A		17.	E
8.	D		18.	A
9.	B		19.	B
10.	A		20.	C

21. E
22. A
23. E
24. E
25. C

EXAMINATION SECTION
TEST 1

DIRECTIONS: In each of the following questions, only one of the four sentences conforms to standards of correct usage. The other three contain errors in grammar, diction, or punctuation. Select the choice in each question which BEST conforms to standards of correct usage. Consider a choice correct if it contains none of the errors mentioned above, even though there may be other ways of expressing the same thought. *PRINT THE LETTER OF THE CORRECT ANSWER IN THE SPACE AT THE RIGHT.*

1. A. Because he was ill was no excuse for his behavior
   B. I insist that he see a lawyer before he goes to trial.
   C. He said "that he had not intended to go."
   D. He wasn't out of the office only three days.

   1.____

2. A. He came to the station and pays a porter to carry his bags into the train.
   B. I should have liked to live in medieval times.
   C. My father was born in Linville. A little country town where everybody knows everyone else.
   D. The car, which is parked across the street, is disabled.

   2.____

3. A. He asked the desk clerk for a clean, quiet, room.
   B. I expected James to be lonesome and that he would want to go home.
   C. I have stopped worrying because I have heard nothing further on the subject.
   D. If the board of directors controls the company, they may take actions which are disapproved by the stockholders.

   3.____

4. A. Each of the players knew their place.
   B. He whom you saw on the stage is the son of an actor.
   C. Susan is the smartest of the twin sisters.
   D. Who ever thought of him winning both prizes?

   4.____

5. A. An outstanding trait of early man was their reliance on omens.
   B. Because I had never been there before.
   C. Neither Mr. Jones nor Mr. Smith has completed his work.
   D. While eating my dinner, a dog came to the window.

   5.____

6. A. A copy of the lease, in addition to the Rules and Regulations, are to be given to each tenant.
   B. The Rules and Regulations and a copy of the lease is being given to each tenant.
   C. A copy of the lease, in addition to the Rules and Regulations, is to be given to each tenant.
   D. A copy of the lease, in addition to the Rules and Regulations, are being given to each tenant.

   6.____

7. A. Although we understood that for him music was a passion, we were disturbed by the fact that he was addicted to sing along with the soloists.
    B. Do you believe that Steven is liable to win a scholarship?
    C. Give the picture to whomever is a connoisseur of art.
    D. Whom do you believe to be the most efficient worker in the office?

    7._____

8. A. Each adult who is sure they know all the answers will some day realize their mistake.
    B. Even the most hardhearted villain would have to feel bad about so horrible a tragedy.
    C. Neither being licensed teachers, both aspirants had to pass rigorous tests before being appointed.
    D. The principal reason why he wanted to be designated was because he had never before been to a convention.

    8._____

9. A. Being that the weather was so inclement, the party has been postponed for at least a month.
    B. He is in New York City only three weeks and he has already seen all the thrilling sights in Manhattan and in the other four boroughs.
    C. If you will look it up in the official directory, which can be consulted in the library during specified hours, you will discover that the chairman and director are Mr. T. Henry Long.
    D. Working hard at college during the day and at the post office during the night, he appeared to his family to be indefatigable.

    9._____

10. A. I would have been happy to oblige you if you only asked me to do it.
    B. The cold weather, as well as the unceasing wind and rain, have made us decide to spend the winter in Florida.
    C. The politician would have been more successful in winning office if he would have been less dogmatic.
    D. These trousers are expensive; however, they will wear well.

    10._____

11. A. All except him wore formal attire at the reception for the ambassador.
    B. If that chair were to be blown off of the balcony, it might injure someone below.
    C. Not a passenger, who was in the crash, survived the impact.
    D. To borrow money off friends is the best way to lose them.

    11._____

12. A. Approaching Manhattan on the ferry boat from Staten Island, an unforgettable sight of the skyscrapers is seen.
    B. Did you see the exhibit of modernistic paintings as yet?
    C. Gesticulating wildly and ranting in stentorian tones, the speaker was the sinecure of all eyes.
    D. The airplane with crew and passengers was lost somewhere in the Pacific Ocean.

    12._____

13.
   A. If one has consistently had that kind of training, it is certainly too late to change your entire method of swimming long distances.
   B. The captain would have been more impressed if you would have been more conscientious in evacuation drills.
   C. The passengers on the stricken ship were all ready to abandon it at the signal.
   D. The villainous shark lashed at the lifeboat with it's tail, trying to upset the rocking boat in order to partake of it's contents.

13.____

14.
   A. As one whose been certified as a professional engineer, I believe that the decision to build a bridge over that harbor is unsound.
   B. Between you and me, this project ought to be completed long before winter arrives.
   C. He fervently hoped that the men would be back at camp and to find them busy at their usual chores.
   D. Much to his surprise, he discovered that the climate of Korea was like his home town.

14.____

15.
   A. An industrious executive is aided, not impeded, by having a hobby which gives him a fresh point of view on life and its problems.
   B. Frequent absence during the calendar year will surely mitigate against the chances of promotion.
   C. He was unable to go to the committee meeting because he was very ill.
   D. Mr. Brown expressed his disapproval so emphatically that his associates were embarassed

15.____

16.
   A. At our next session, the office manager will have told you something about his duties and responsibilities.
   B. In general, the book is absorbing and original and have no hesitation about recommending it.
   C. The procedures followed by private industry in dealing with lateness and absence are different from ours.
   D. We shall treat confidentially any information about Mr. Doe, to whom we understand you have sent reports to for many years.

16.____

17.
   A. I talked to one official, whom I knew was fully impartial.
   B. Everyone signed the petition but him.
   C. He proved not only to be a good student but also a good athlete.
   D. All are incorrect.

17.____

18.
   A. Every year a large amount of tenants are admitted to housing projects.
   B. Henry Ford owned around a billion dollars in industrial equipment.
   C. He was aggravated by the child's poor behavior.
   D. All are incorrect.

18.____

19. A. Before he was committed to the asylum he suffered from the illusion that he was Napoleon.
    B. Besides stocks, there were also bonds in the safe.
    C. We bet the other team easily.
    D. All are incorrect.

20. A. Bring this report to your supervisory.
    B. He set the chair down near the table.
    C. The capitol of New York is Albany.
    D. All are incorrect.

21. A. He was chosen to arbitrate the dispute because everyone knew he would be disinterested.
    B. It is advisable to obtain the best council before making an important decision.
    C. Less college students are interested in teaching than ever before.
    D. All are incorrect.

22. A. She, hearing a signal, the source lamp flashed.
    B. While hearing a signal, the source lamp flashed.
    C. In hearing a signal, the source lamp flashed.
    D. As she heard a signal, the source lamp flashed.

23. A. Every one of the time records have been initialed in the designated spaces.
    B. All of the time records has been initialed in the designated spaces.
    C. Each one of the time records was initialed in the designated spaces.
    D. The time records all been initialed in the designated spaces.

24. A. If there is no one else to answer the phone, you will have to answer it.
    B. You will have to answer it yourself if no one else answers the phone.
    C. If no one else is not around to pick up the phone, you will have to do it.
    D. You will have to answer the phone when nobodys here to do it.

25. A. Dr. Barnes not in his office. What could I do for you?
    B. Dr. Barnes is not in his office. Is there something I can do for you?
    C. Since Dr. Barnes is not in his office, might there be something I may do for you?
    D. Is there any ways I can assist you since Dr. Barnes is not in his office?

26. A. She do not understand how the new console works.
    B. The way the new console works, she doesn't understand.
    C. She doesn't understand how the new console works.
    D. The new console works, so that she doesn't understand.

27. A. Certain changes in my family income must be reported as they occur.
    B. When certain changes in family income occur, it must be reported.
    C. Certain family income change must be reported as they occur.
    D. Certain changes in family income must be reported as they have been occurring.

28. A. Each tenant has to complete the application themselves.
    B. Each of the tenants have to complete the application by himself.
    C. Each of the tenants has to complete the application himself.
    D. Each of the tenants has to complete the application by themselves.

28._____

29. A. Yours is the only building that the construction will effect.
    B. Your's is the only building affected by the construction.
    C. The construction will only effect your building.
    D. Yours is the only building that will be affected by the construction.

29._____

30. A. There is four tests left.
    B. The number of tests left are four.
    C. There are four tests left.
    D. Four of the tests remains.

30._____

31. A. Each of the applicants takes a test.
    B. Each of the applicant take a test.
    C. Each of the applicants take tests.
    D. Each of the applicants have taken tests.

31._____

32. A. The applicant, not the examiners, are ready.
    B. The applicants, not the examiners, is ready.
    C. The applicants, not the examiner, are ready.
    D. The applicant, not the examiner, are ready

32._____

33. A. You will not progress except you practice.
    B. You will not progress without you practicing.
    C. You will not progress unless you practice.
    D. You will not progress provided you do not practice.

33._____

34. A. Neither the director or the employees will be at the office tomorrow.
    B. Neither the director nor the employees will be at the office tomorrow.
    C. Neither the director, or the secretary nor the other employees will be at the office tomorrow.
    D. Neither the director, the secretary or the other employees will be at the office tomorrow.

34._____

35. A. In my absence, he and her will have to finish the assignment.
    B. In my absence he and she will have to finish the assignment.
    C. In my absence she and him, they will have to finish the assignment.
    D. In my absence he and her both will have to finish the assignment.

35._____

KEY (CORRECT ANSWERS)

1.	B	11.	A	21.	A	31.	A
2.	B	12.	D	22.	D	32.	C
3.	C	13.	C	23.	C	33.	C
4.	B	14.	B	24.	A	34.	B
5.	C	15.	A	25.	B	35.	B
6.	C	16.	C	26.	C		
7.	D	17.	B	27.	A		
8.	B	18.	D	28.	C		
9.	D	19.	B	29.	D		
10.	D	20.	B	30.	C		

TEST 2

DIRECTIONS: Each question or incomplete statement is followed by several suggested answers or completions. Select the one that BEST answers the question or completes the statement. *PRINT THE LETTER OF THE CORRECT ANSWER IN THE SPACE AT THE RIGHT.*

Questions 1-4.

DIRECTIONS: Questions 1 through 4 consist of three sentences each. For each question, select the sentence which contains NO error in grammar or usage.

1. A. Be sure that everybody brings his notes to the conference.
    B. He looked like he meant to hit the boy.
    C. Mr. Jones is one of the clients who was chosen to represent the district.
    D. All are incorrect.

2. A. He is taller than I.
    B. I'll have nothing to do with these kind of people.
    C. The reason why he will not buy the house is because it is too expensive.
    D. All are incorrect.

3. A. Aren't I eligible for this apartment.
    B. Have you seen him anywheres?
    C. He should of come earlier.
    D. All are incorrect.

4. A. He graduated college in 2022.
    B. He hadn't but one more line to write.
    C. Who do you think is the author of this report?
    D. All are incorrect.

Questions 5-35.

DIRECTIONS: In each of the following questions, only one of the four sentences conforms to standards of correct usage. The other three contain errors in grammar, diction, or punctuation. Select the choice in each question which BEST conforms to standards of correct usage. Consider a choice correct if it contains none of the errors mentioned above, even though there may be other ways of expressing the same thought.

5. A. It is obvious that no one wants to be a kill-joy if they can help it.
    B. It is not always possible, and perhaps it never ispossible, to judge a person's character by just looking at him.
    C. When Yogi Berra of the New York Yankees hit an immortal grandslam home run, everybody in the huge stadium including Pittsburgh fans, rose to his feet.
    D. Every one of us students must pay tuition today.

6. A. The physician told the young mother that if the baby is not able to digest its milk, it should be boiled.
    B. There is no doubt whatsoever that he felt deeply hurt because John Smith had betrayed the trust.
    C. Having partaken of a most delicious repast prepared by Tessie Breen, the hostess, the horses were driven home immediately thereafter.
    D. The attorney asked my wife and myself several questions.

    6._____

7. A. Despite all denials, there is no doubt in my mind that
    B. At this time everyone must deprecate the demogogic attack made by one of our Senators on one of our most revered statesmen.
    C. In the first game of a crucial two-game series, Ted Williams, got two singles, both of them driving in a run.
    D. Our visitor brought good news to John and I.

    7._____

8. A. If he would have told me, I should have been glad to help him in his dire financial emergency.
    B. Newspaper men have often asserted that diplomats or so-called official spokesmen sometimes employ equivocation in attempts to deceive.
    C. I think someones coming to collect money for the Red Cross.
    D. In a masterly summation, the young attorney expressed his belief that the facts clearly militate against this opinion.

    8._____

9. A. We have seen most all the exhibits.
    B. Without in the least underestimating your advice, in my opinion the situation has grown immeasurably worse in the past few days.
    C. I wrote to the box office treasurer of the hit show that a pair of orchestra seats would be preferable.
    D. As the grim story of Pearl Harbor was broadcast on that fateful December 7, it was the general opinion that war was inevitable.

    9._____

10. A. Without a moment's hesitation, Casey Stengel said that Larry Berra works harder than any player on the team.
    B. There is ample evidence to indicate that many animals can run faster than any human being.
    C. No one saw the accident but I.
    D. Example of courage is the heroic defense put up by the paratroopers against overwhelming odds.

    10._____

11. A. If you prefer these kind, Mrs. Grey, we shall be more than willing to let you have them reasonably.
    B. If you like these here, Mrs. Grey, we shall be more than willing to let you have them reasonably.
    C. If you like these, Mrs. Grey, we shall be more than willing to let you have them.
    D. Who shall we appoint?

    11._____

3 (#2)

12.
   A. The number of errors are greater in speech than in writing.
   B. The doctor rather than the nurse was to blame for his being neglected.
   C. Because the demand for these books have been so great, we reduced the price.
   D. John Galsworthy, the English novelist, could not have survived a serious illness; had it not been for loving care.

   12.____

13.
   A. Our activities this year have seldom ever been as interesting as they have been this month.
   B. Our activities this month have been more interesting, or at least as interesting as those of any month this year.
   C. Our activities this month has been more interesting than those of any other month this year.
   D. Neither Jean nor her sister was at home.

   13.____

14.
   A. George B. Shaw's view of common morality, as well as his wit sparkling with a dash of perverse humor here and there, have led critics to term him "The Incurable Rebel."
   B. The President's program was not always received with the wholehearted endorsement of his own party, which is why the party faces difficulty in drawing up a platform for the coming election.
   C. The reason why they wanted to travel was because they had never been away from home.
   D. Facing a barrage of cameras, the visiting celebrity found it extremely difficult to express his opinions clearly.

   14.____

15.
   A. When we calmed down, we all agreed that our anger had been kind of unnecessary and had not helped the situation.
   B. Without him going into all the details, he made us realize the horror of the accident.
   C. Like one girl, for example, who applied for two positions.
   D. Do not think that you have to be so talented as he is in order to play in the school orchestra.

   15.____

16.
   A. He looked very peculiarly to me.
   B. He certainly looked at me peculiar.
   C. Due to the train's being late, we had to wait an hour.
   D. The reason for the poor attendance is that it is raining.

   16.____

17.
   A. About one out of four own an automobile.
   B. The collapse of the old Mitchell Bridge was caused by defective construction in the central pier.
   C. Brooks Atkinson was well acquainted with the best literature, thus helping him to become an able critic.
   D. He has to stand still until the relief man comes up, thus giving him no chance to move about and keep warm.

   17.____

18. A. He is sensitive to confusion and withdraws from people whom he feels are too noisy.
    B. Do you know whether the data is statistically correct?
    C. Neither the mayor or the aldermen are to blame.
    D. Of those who were graduated from high school, a goodly percentage went to college.

18.____

19. A. Acting on orders, the offices were searched by a designated committee.
    B. The answer probably is nothing.
    C. I thought it to be all right to excuse them from class.
    D. I think that he is as successful a singer, if not more successful, than Mary.

19.____

20. A. $360,000 is really very little to pay for such a wellbuilt house.
    B. The creatures looked like they had come from outer space.
    C. It was her, he knew!
    D. Nobody but me knows what to do.

20.____

21. A. Mrs. Smith looked good in her new suit.
    B. New York may be compared with Chicago.
    C. I will not go to the meeting except you go with me.
    D. I agree with this editorial.

21.____

22. A. My opinions are different from his.
    B. There will be less students in class now.
    C. Helen was real glad to find her watch.
    D. It had been pushed off of her dresser.

22.____

23. A. Almost everyone, who has been to California, returns with glowing reports.
    B. George Washington, John Adams, and Thomas Jefferson, were our first presidents.
    C. Mr. Walters, whom we met at the bank yesterday, is the man, who gave me my first job.
    D. One should study his lessons as carefully as he can.

23.____

24. A. We had such a good time yesterday.
    B. When the bell rang, the boys and girls went in the schoolhouse.
    C. John had the worst headache when he got up this morning.
    D. Today's assignment is somewhat longer than yesterday's.

24.____

25. A. Neither the mayor nor the city clerk are willing to talk.
    B. Neither the mayor nor the city clerk is willing to talk.
    C. Neither the mayor or the city clerk are willing to talk.
    D Neither the mayor or the city clerk is willing to talk.

25.____

26. A. Being that he is that kind of boy, cooperation cannot be expected.
    B. He interviewed people who he thought had something to say.
    C. Stop whomever enters the building regardless of rank or office held.
    D. Passing through the countryside, the scenery pleased us.

26.____

27. A. The childrens' shoes were in their closet.
    B. The children's shoes were in their closet.
    C. The childs' shoes were in their closet.
    D. The childs' shoes were in his closet.

27.____

28. A. An agreement was reached between the defendant, the plaintiff, the plaintiff's attorney and the insurance company as to the amount of the settlement.
    B. Everybody was asked to give their versions of the accident.
    C. The consensus of opinion was that the evidence was inconclusive.
    D. The witness stated that if he was rich, he wouldn't have had to loan the money.

28.____

29. A. Before beginning the investigation, all the materials related to the case were carefully assembled.
    B. The reason for his inability to keep the appointment is because of his injury in the accident.
    C. This here evidence tends to support the claim of the defendant.
    D. We interviewed all the witnesses who, according to the driver, were still in town.

29.____

30. A. Each claimant was allowed the full amount of their medical expenses.
    B. Either of the three witnesses is available.
    C. Every one of the witnesses was asked to tell his story.
    D. Neither of the witnesses are right.

30.____

31. A. The commissioner, as well as his deputy and various bureau heads, were present.
    B. A new organization of employers and employees have been formed.
    C. One or the other of these men have been selected.
    D. The number of pages in the book is enough to discourage a reader.

31.____

32. A. Between you and me, I think he is the better man.
    B. He was believed to be me.
    C. Is it us that you wish to see?
    D. The winners are him and her.

32.____

33. A. Beside the statement to the police, the witness spoke to no one.
    B. He made no statement other than to the police and I.
    C. He made no statement to any one else, aside from the police.
    D. The witness spoke to no one but me.

33.____

34. A. The claimant has no one to blame but himself.
    B. The boss sent us, he and I, to deliver the packages.
    C. The lights come from mine and not his car.
    D. There was room on the stairs for him and myself.

34.____

35. A. Admission to this clinic is limited to patients' inability to pay for medical care.
     B. Patients who can pay little or nothing for medical care are treated in this clinic.
     C. The patient's ability to pay for medical care is the determining factor in his admission to this clinic.
     D. This clinic is for the patient's that cannot afford to pay or that can pay a little for medical care.

35._____

KEY (CORRECT ANSWERS)

1.	A	11.	C	21.	A	31.	D
2.	A	12.	B	22.	A	32.	A
3.	D	13.	D	23.	D	33.	D
4.	C	14.	D	24.	D	34.	A
5.	D	15.	D	25.	B	35.	B
6.	D	16.	D	26.	B		
7.	B	17.	B	27.	B		
8.	B	18.	D	28.	C		
9.	D	19.	B	29.	D		
10.	B	20.	D	30.	C		

ARITHMETICAL REASONING
EXAMINATION SECTION
TEST 1

DIRECTIONS: Each question or incomplete statement is followed by several suggested answers or completions. Select the one that BEST answers the question or completes the statement. *PRINT THE LETTER OF THE CORRECT ANSWER IN THE SPACE AT THE RIGHT.*

1. If a secretary answered 28 phone calls and typed the addresses for 112 credit statements in one morning, what is the RATIO of phone calls answered to credit statements typed for that period of time?

    A. 1:4   B. 1:7   C. 2:3   D. 3:5

2. According to a suggested filing system, no more than 10 folders should be filed behind any one file guide and from 15 to 25 file guides should be used in each file drawer for easy finding and filing.
    The MAXIMUM number of folders that a five-drawer file cabinet can hold to allow easy finding and filing is

    A. 550   B. 750   C. 1,100   D. 1,250

3. An employee had a starting salary of $19,353. He received a salary increase at the end of each year, and at the end of the seventh year his salary was $25,107.
    What was his AVERAGE annual increase in salary over these seven years?

    A. $765   B. $807   C. $822   D. $858

4. The 55 typists and 28 senior clerks in a certain agency were paid a total of $1,457,400 in salaries in 2005.
    If the average annual salary of a typist was $16,800, the average annual salary of a senior clerk was

    A. $19,050   B. $19,950   C. $20,100   D. $20,250

5. A typist has been given a three-page report to type. She has finished typing the first two pages. The first page has 283 words, and the second page has 366 words.
    If the total report consists of 954 words, how many words will she have to type on the third page of the report?

    A. 202   B. 287   C. 305   D. 313

6. In one day, Clerk A processed 30% more forms than Clerk B, and Clerk C processed 1 1/4 as many forms as Clerk A.
    If Clerk B processed 40 forms, how many more forms were processed by Clerk C than Clerk B?

    A. 12   B. 13   C. 21   D. 25

7. A clerk who earns a gross salary of $678 every 2 weeks has the following deductions taken from her paycheck: 15% for city, state, and federal taxes; 2 1/2% for Social Security; $1.95 for health insurance; and $9.00 for union dues.
The amount of her take-home pay is

   A. $429.60   B. $468.60   C. $497.40   D. $548.40

8. In 2002, an agency spent $400 to buy pencils at a cost of $1.00 a dozen.
If the agency used 3/4 of these pencils in 2002 and used the same number of pencils in 2003, how many more pencils did it have to buy to have enough pencils for all of 2003?

   A. 1,200   B. 2,400   C. 3,600   D. 4,800

9. A clerk who worked in Agency X earned the following salaries: $15,105 the first year, $15,750 the second year, and $16,440 the third year. Another clerk who worked in Agency Y for three years earned $15,825 a year for two years and $16,086 the third year. The DIFFERENCE between the average salaries received by both clerks over a three-year period is

   A. $147   B. $153   C. $261   D. $423

10. An employee who works more than 40 hours in any week receives overtime payment for the extra hours at time and one-half (1 1/2 times) his hourly rate of pay. An employee who earns $13.60 an hour works a total of 45 hours during a certain week.
His TOTAL pay for that week would be

    A. $564.40   B. $612.00   C. $646.00   D. $824.00

11. Suppose that the amount of money spent for supplies in 2006 for a division in a city department was $156,500. This represented an increase of 12% over the amount spent for supplies for this division in 2005.
The amount of money spent for supplies for this division in 2005 was MOST NEARLY

    A. $139,730   B. $137,720   C. $143,460   D. $138,720

12. Suppose that a group of five clerks have been assigned to insert 24,000 letters into envelopes. The clerks perform this work at the following rates of speed: Clerk A, 1,100 letters an hour; Clerk B, 1,450 letters an hour; Clerk C, 1,200 letters an hour; Clerk D, 1,300 letters an hour; Clerk E, 1,250 letters an hour. At the end of two hours of work, Clerks C and D are assigned to another task.
From the time that Clerks C and D were taken off the assignment, the number of hours required for the remaining clerks to complete this assignment is

    A. less than 3 hours
    B. 3 hours
    C. more than 3 hours, but less than 4 hours
    D. more than 4 hours

13. The number 60 is 40% of

    A. 24   B. 84   C. 96   D. 150

14. If 3/8 of a number is 96, the number is

    A. 132   B. 36   C. 256   D. 156

15. A city department uses an average of 25 20-cent, 35 30-cent, and 350 40-cent postage stamps each day.
The TOTAL cost of stamps used by the department in a five-day period is

   A. $29.50 B. $155.50 C. $290.50 D. $777.50

16. A city department issued 12,000 applications in 2000. The number of applications that the department issued in 1998 was 25% greater than the number it issued in 2000.
If the department issued 10% fewer applications in 1996 than it did in 1998, the number it issued in 1996 was

   A. 16,500 B. 13,500 C. 9,900 D. 8,100

17. A clerk can add 40 columns of figures an hour by using an adding machine and 20 columns of figures an hour without using an adding machine.
The TOTAL number of hours it would take him to add 200 columns if he does 3/5 of the work by machine and the rest without the machine is

   A. 6 B. 7 C. 8 D. 9

18. In 1997, a city department bought 500 dozen pencils at $1.20 per dozen. In 2000, only 75 percent as many pencils were bought as were bought in 1997, but the price was 20 percent higher than the 1997 price. The TOTAL cost of the pencils bought in 2000 was

   A. $540 B. $562.50 C. $720 D. $750

19. A clerk is assigned to check the accuracy of the entries on 490 forms. He checks 40 forms an hour. After working one hour on this task, he is joined by another clerk, who checks these forms at the rate of 35 an hour.
The TOTAL number of hours required to do the entire assignment is

   A. 5 B. 6 C. 7 D. 8

20. Assume that there are a total of 420 employees in a city agency. Thirty percent of the employees are clerks, and 1/7 are typists.
The DIFFERENCE between the number of clerks and the number of typists is

   A. 126 B. 66 C. 186 D. 80

21. Assume that a duplicating machine produces copies of a bulletin at a cost of 2 cents per copy. The machine produces 120 copies of the bulletin per minute.
If the cost of producing a certain number of copies was $12, how many minutes of operation did it take the machine to produce this number of copies?

   A. 5 B. 2 C. 10 D. 6

22. An assignment is completed by 32 clerks in 22 days. Assuming that all the clerks work at the same rate of speed, the number of clerks that would be needed to complete this assignment in 16 days is

   A. 27 B. 38 C. 44 D. 52

23. A department head hired a total of 60 temporary employees to handle a seasonal increase in the department's workload. The following lists the number of temporary employees hired, their rates of pay, and the duration of their employment:
   One-third of the total were hired as clerks, each at the rate of $27,500 a year, for two months.
   30 percent of the total were hired as office machine operators, each at the rate of $31,500 a year, for four months.
   22 stenographers were hired, each at the rate of $30,000 a year, for three months.
The total amount paid to these temporary employees was MOST NEARLY

   A. $1,780,000   B. $450,000
   C. $650,000   D. $390,000

24. Assume that there are 2,300 employees in a city agency. Also, assume that five percent of these employees are accountants, that 80 percent of the accountants have college degrees, and that one-half of the accountants who have college degrees have five years of experience. Then, the number of employees in the agency who are accountants with college degrees and five years of experience is

   A. 46   B. 51   C. 460   D. 920

25. Assume that the regular 8-hour working day of a laborer is from 8 A.M. to 5 P.M., with an hour off for lunch. He earns a regular hourly rate of pay for these 8 hours and is paid at the rate of time-and-a-half for each hour worked after his regular working day.
If, on a certain day, he works from 8 A.M. to 6 P.M., with an hour off for lunch, and earns $171, his regular hourly rate of pay is

   A. $16.30   B. $17.10   C. $18.00   D. $19.00

KEY (CORRECT ANSWERS)

1. A
2. D
3. C
4. A
5. C
6. D
7. D
8. B
9. A
10. C

11. A
12. B
13. D
14. C
15. D
16. B
17. B
18. A
19. C
20. B

21. A
22. C
23. B
24. A
25. C

SOLUTIONS TO PROBLEMS

1. 28/112 is equivalent to 1:4

2. Maximum number of folders = (10)(25)(5) = 1250

3. Average annual increase = ($25,107-19,353) ÷ 7 = $822

4. $1,457,400 - (55)($16,800) = $533,400 = total amount paid to senior clerks. Average senior clerk's salary = $533,400 ÷ 28 = $19,050

5. Number of words on 3rd page = 954 - 283 - 366 = 305

6. Clerk A processed (40)(1.30) = 52 forms and clerk C processed (52)(1.25) = 65 forms. Finally, 65 - 40 = 25

7. Take-home pay = $678 - (.15)($678) - (.025)($678) - $1.95 - $9.00 = $548.40

8. (400)(12) = 4800 pencils. In 2002, (3/4)(4800) = 3600 were used, so that 1200 pencils were available at the beginning of 2003. Since 3600 pencils were also used in 2003, the agency had to buy 3600 - 1200 = 2400 pencils.

9. Average salary for clerk in Agency X = ($15,105+$15,750+$16,440)/3 = $15,765. Average salary for clerk in Agency Y = ($15,825+ $15,825+$16,086) ÷ 3 = $15,912. Difference in average salaries = $147.

10. Total pay = ($13.60)(40) + ($20.40)(5) = $646.00

11. In 2005, amount spent = $156,500 ÷ 1.12 ≈ $139,730 (Actual value = $139,732.1429)

12. At the end of 2 hours, (1100)(2) + (1450)(2) + (1200)(2) + (1300X2) + (1250X2) = 12,600 letters have been inserted into envelopes. The remaining 11,400 letters done by clerks A, B, and C will require 11,400 ÷ (1100+1450+1250) = 3 hours.

13. 60 ÷ .40 = 150

14. 96 ÷ 3/8 = (96)(8/3) = 256

15. Total cost = (5)[(25)(.20)+(35)(.30)+(350)(.40)]= $777.50

16. In 1998, (12,000) (1.25) = 15,000 applications were issued In 1996, (15,000)(.90) = 13,500 applications were issued

17. Total number of hours $=\dfrac{120}{40} + \dfrac{80}{20} = 7$

18. (.75)(500 dozen) = 375 dozen purchased in 2000 at a cost of ($1.20)(1.20) = $1.44 per dozen. Total cost for 2000 = ($1.44) (375) = $540

19. Total time = 1 hour + 450/75 hrs. = 7 hours

20. (.30)(420) - (1/7)(420) = 126 - 60 = 66

21. Cost per minute = (120)(.02) = $2.40. Then, $12 ÷ $2.40 = 5 minutes

22. (32)(22) ÷ 16 = 44 clerks

23. Total amount paid = (20)($27,500)(2/12) + (18)($31,500)(4/12) + (22)($30,000)(3/12) = $445,666.$\overline{6}$ ≈ $450,000

24. Number of accountants with college degrees and five years of experience = (2300)(.05)(.80)(1/2) = 46

25. Let x = regular hourly pay. Then, (8)(x) + (1)(1.5x) = $1.71 So, 9.5$x$ = 171. Solving, x = $18

TEST 2

DIRECTIONS: Each question or incomplete statement is followed by several suggested answers or completions. Select the one that BEST answers the question or completes the statement. *PRINT THE LETTER OF THE CORRECT ANSWER IN THE SPACE AT THE RIGHT.*

1. Assume that you know the capacity of a filing cabinet, the extent of which it is filled, and the daily rate at which material is being added to the file.
In order to estimate how many more days it will take for the cabinet to be filled to capacity, you should

    A. divide the extent to which the cabinet is filled by the daily rate
    B. take the difference between the capacity of the cabinet and the material in it, and multiply the result by the daily rate of adding material
    C. divide the daily rate of adding material by the difference between the capacity of the cabinet and the material in it
    D. take the difference between the capacity of the cabinet and the material in it, and divide the result by the daily rate of adding material

1.____

2. Suppose you have been asked to compute the average salary earned in your department during the past year. For each of the divisions of the department, you are given the number of employees and the average salary.
In order to find the requested overall average salary for the department, you should

    A. add the average salaries of the various divisions and divide the total by the number of divisions
    B. multiply the number of employees in each division by the corresponding average salary, add the results and divide the total by the number of employees in the department
    C. add the average salaries of the various divisions and divide the total by the total number of employees in the department
    D. multiply the sum of the average salaries of the various divisions by the total number of divisions and divide the resulting product by the total number of employees in the department

2.____

3. Suppose that a group of six clerks has been assigned to assemble the duplicated pages of a report into completed copies. After four hours of work, they have been able to complete one-third of the job.
In order to assemble all the remaining copies in three more hours of work, the number of clerks which will have to be added to the original six, assuming that all the clerks assigned to this task work at the same rate of speed, is

    A. 10   B. 16   C. 2   D. 6

3.____

4. A study of the grades of students in a certain college revealed that in 2005, 15% fewer students received a passing grade in mathematics than in 2004, whereas in 2006 the number of students passing mathematics increased 15% over 2005.
On the basis of this study, it would be MOST accurate to conclude that

    A. the same percentage of students passed mathematics in 2004 as in 2006
    B. of the three years studied, the greatest percentage of students passed mathematics in 2006

4.____

C. the percentage of students who passed mathematics in 2006 was less than the percentage passing this subject in 2004
D. the percentage of students passing mathematics in 2004 was 15% greater than the percentage of students passing this subject in 2006

5. A city department employs 1,400 people, of whom 35% are clerks and 1/8 are stenographers.
   The number of employees in the department who are neither clerks nor stenographers is

   A. 640   B. 665   C. 735   D. 760

6. Assume that there are 190 papers to be filed and that Clerk A and Clerk B are assigned to file these papers. If Clerk A files 40 papers more than Clerk B, then the number of papers that Clerk A files is

   A. 75   B. 110   C. 115   D. 150

7. A stock clerk had on hand the following items:
   500 pads, each worth 16 cents
   130 pencils, each worth 12 cents
   50 dozen rubber bands, worth 8 cents a dozen
   If, from this stock, he issued 125 pads, 45 pencils, and 48 rubber bands, the value of the remaining stock would be

   A. $25.72   B. $27.80   C. $70.52   D. $73.88

8. In a particular agency, there were 160 accidents in 2002. Of these accidents, 75% were due to unsafe acts and the rest were due to unsafe conditions. In the following year, a special safety program was established. The number of accidents in 2004 due to unsafe acts was reduced to 35% of what it had been in 2002.
   How many accidents due to unsafe acts were there in 2004?

   A. 20   B. 36   C. 42   D. 56

9. At the end of every month, the petty cash fund of Agency A is reimbursed for payments made from the fund during the month. During the month of February, the amounts paid from the fund were entered on receipts as follows: 10 bus fares of $1.40 each and one taxi fare of $14.00. At the end of the month, the money left in the fund was in the following denominations: 60 one-dollar bills, 16 quarters, 40 dimes, and 80 nickels.
   If the petty cash fund is reduced by 20% for the following month, how much money will there be available in the petty cash fund for March?

   A. $44   B. $80   C. $86   D. $100

10. An employee worked on a job for 6 weeks, 5 days per week, and 8 hours per day. How many hours did he work on the job?

    A. 40   B. 48   C. 55   D. 240

11. Divide 35 by .7.

    A. 5   B. 42   C. 50   D. 245

12. .1% of 25 =

    A. .025   B. .25   C. 2.5   D. 25

13. In a city agency, 80 percent of the total number of employees are more than 25 years of age and 65 percent of the total number of employees are high school graduates.
    The SMALLEST possible percent of employees who are both high school graduates and more than 25 years of age is

    A. 35%   B. 45%   C. 55%   D. 65%

14. Two clerical units, X and Y, each having a different number of clerks, are assigned to file registration cards. It takes Unit X, which contains 8 clerks, 21 days to file the same number of cards that Unit Y can file in 28 days. It is also a fact that Unit X can file 174,528 cards in 72 days.
    Assuming that all the clerks in both units work at the same rate of speed, the number of cards which can be filed by Unit Y in 144 days, if 4 more clerks are added to the staff of Unit Y, is MOST NEARLY

    A. 392,000   B. 436,000   C. 523,000   D. 669,000

15. Assume that two machines, each costing $14,750, were purchased for your office. Each machine requires the services of an operator at a salary of $2,000 per month. These machines are to replace six clerks, two of whom earn $1,550 per month each, and four of whom earn $1,700 per month each.
    The number of months it will take for the cost of the machines to be made up from the savings in salaries is

    A. less than four   B. four
    C. five   D. more than five

16. Suppose that the amount of stationery used by your department in August decreased by 16% as compared with the amount used in July, and that the amount used in September increased by 25% as compared with the amount used in August.
    The amount of stationery used in September as compared with the amount used in July is

    A. greater by 5 percent   B. less by 5 percent
    C. greater by 9 percent   D. the same

17. An employee earns $48 a day and works 5 days a week.
    He will earn $2,160 in _____ weeks.

    A. 5   B. 7   C. 8   D. 9

18. In a certain bureau, the entire staff consists of 1 senior supervisor, 2 supervisors, 6 assistant supervisors, and 54 associate workers.
    The percent of the staff who are not associate workers is MOST NEARLY

    A. 14   B. 21   C. 27   D. 32

19. In a certain bureau, five employees each earn $1,000 a month, another 3 employees each earn $2,200 a month, and another two employees each earn $1,400 a month.
    The monthly payroll for these employees is

    A. $3,600   B. $8,800   C. $11,400   D. $14,400

20. An employee contributes 5% of his salary to the pension fund. If his salary is $1,200 a month, the amount of his contribution to the pension fund in a year is

   A. $480 B. $720 C. $960 D. $1,200

21. The number of square feet in an area that is 50 feet long and 30 feet wide is

   A. 80 B. 150 C. 800 D. 1,500

22. A farm hand was paid a weekly wage of $332.16 for a 48-hour work week. As a result of a new labor contract, he is paid $344.96 a week for a 44-hour work week with time and one-half pay for time worked in excess of 44 hours in any work week.
    If he continues to work 48 hours weekly under the new contract, the amount by which his average hourly rate for a 48-hour work week under the new contract exceeds the hourly rate previously paid him lies between _____ and _____ cents, inclusive.

   A. 91;100 B. 101;110 C. 111;120 D. 121;130

23. Each side of a square room, which is being used as an office, measures 66 feet. The floor of the room is divided by six traffic aisles, each aisle being six feet wide. Three of the aisles run parallel to the east and west sides of the room, and the other three run parallel to the north and south sides of the room, so that the remaining floor space is divided into 16 equal sections. If all of the floor space which is not being used for traffic aisles is occupied by desk and chair sets, and each set takes up 24 square feet of floor space, the number of desk and chair sets in the room is

   A. 80 B. 64 C. 36 D. 96

24. In 2005, a city agency bought 12,000 envelopes at $4.00 per hundred. In 2006, the price of envelopes purchased was 40 percent higher than the 2005 price, but only 60 percent as many envelopes were bought.
    The total cost of the envelopes purchased in 2006 was MOST NEARLY

   A. $250 B. $320 C. $400 D. $480

25. In a city agency, 25 percent of the women employees and 50 percent of the men employees attended a general staff meeting.
    If 48 percent of all the employees in the agency are women, the percentage of all the employees who attended the meeting is

   A. 36% B. 37% C. 38% D. 75%

KEY (CORRECT ANSWERS)

1. D
2. B
3. A
4. C
5. C

6. C
7. D
8. C
9. B
10. D

11. C
12. A
13. B
14. A
15. C

16. A
17. D
18. A
19. D
20. B

21. D
22. D
23. D
24. C
25. C

SOLUTIONS TO PROBLEMS

1. To determine number of days required to fill cabinet to capacity, subtract material in it from capacity amount, then divide by daily rate of adding material. Example: A cabinet already has 10 folders in it, and the capacity is 100 folders. Suppose 5 folders per day are added. Number of days to fill to capacity = (100-10) ÷ 5 = 18

2. To determine overall average salary, multiply number of employees in each division by that division's average salary, add results, then divide by total number of employees. Example: Division A has 4 employees with average salary of $40,000; division B has 6 employees with average salary of $36,000; division C has 2 employees with average salary of $46,000. Average salary = [(4)($40,000)+(6)($36,000)+(2)($46,000)] / 12 = $39,000

3. (6)(4) = 24 clerk-hours. Since only one-third of work has been done, (24) (3) - 24 = 48 clerk-hours remain. Then, 48 3 = 16 clerks. Thus, 16 - 6 = 10 additional clerks.

4. The percentage of students passing math in 2006 was less than the percentage of those passing math in 2004. Example: Suppose 400 students passed math in 2004. Then, (400)(.85) = 340 passed in 2005. Finally, (340)(1.15) = 391 passed in 2006.

5. 1400 - (.35)(1400) - (1/8)(1400) = 735

6. Let x = number of papers filed by clerk A, x-40 = number of papers filed by clerk B. Then, x + (x-40) = 190 Solving, x = 115

7. (500-125)(.16) + (130-45)(.12) + (50 - 48/12)(.08) = $60.00 + $10.20 + $3.68 = $73.88

8. (160)(.75) = 120 accidents due to unsafe acts in 2002. In 2004, (120)(.35) = 42 accidents due to unsafe acts

9. Original amount at beginning of February in the fund = (10)($1.40) + (1)($14.00) + (60)($1) + (16)(.25) + (40)(.10) + (80)(.05) = $100. Finally, for March, ($100)(.80) = $80 will be available

10. Total hours = (6)(5)(8) = 240

11. 35 ÷ .7 = 50

12. .1% of 25 = (.001)(25) = .025

13. Let A = percent of employees who are at least 25 years old and B = percent of employees who are high school graduates. Also, let N = percent of employees who fit neither category and J = percent of employees who are in both categories. Then, 100 = A + B + N - J. Substituting, 100 = 80 + 65 + N - J To minimize J, let N = 0. So, 100 = 80 + 65 + 0 - J. Solving, J = 45

14. Let Y = number of clerks in Unit Y. Then, (8)(21) = (4)(28), so Y = 6. Unit X has 8 clerks who can file 174,528 cards in 72 flays; thus, each clerk in Unit X can file 174,528 ÷ 72 ÷ 8 = 303 cards per day. Adding 4 clerks to Unit Y will yield 10 clerks in that unit. Since their rate is equal to that of Unit X, the clerks in Unit Y will file, in 144 days, is (303)(10)(144) = 436,320 ≈ 436,000 cards.

15. Let x = required number of months. The cost of the machines in x months = (2)(14,750) + (2)(2000)(x) = 29,500 + 4000x. The savings in salaries for the displaced clerks = x[(2)(1550) +(4)(1700)] = 9900x. Thus, 29,500 + 4000x = 9900x. Solving, x = 5. So, five months will elapse in order to achieve a savings in cost.

16. Let x = amount used in July, so that .84x = amount used in August. For September, the amount used = (.84x)(1.25) = 1.05x. This means the amount used in September is 5% more than the amount used in July.

17. Each week he earns ($48)(5) = $240. Then, $2160 ÷ $240 = 9 weeks

18. (1+2+6) ÷ 63 = 1/7 ≈ 14%

19. Monthly payroll = (5)($1000) + (3)($2200) + (2)($1400) = $14,400

20. Yearly contribution to pension fund = (12)($1200)(.05) = $720

21. (50')(30') = 1500 sq.ft.

22. Old rate = 332.16 ÷ 48 = 6.92 (48 hours)
    New rate = 344.96 (44 hours)
    Overtime rate = 344.96 ÷ 44 = 7.75/hr. x 1.5 x 4 = 46.48
    344.96 + 46.48 = 391.44
    391.44 ÷ 48 = 8.15
    815 - 692 = 123 cents an hour more

23. Each of the 16 sections is a square with side [66'-(3)(6')] ÷ 4 = 12'. So each section contains (12')(12') = 144 sq.ft.
    The number of desk and chair sets = (144 ÷ 24) (16) = 96

24. In 2006, (.60)(12,000) = 7200 envelopes were bought and the price per hundred was ($4.00)(1.40) = $5.60. The total cost = (5.60)(72) = $403.20 ≈ $400

25. (.25)(.48) + (.50)(.52) = .38 = 38%

TEST 3

DIRECTIONS: Each question or incomplete statement is followed by several suggested answers or completions. Select the one that BEST answers the question or completes the statement. *PRINT THE LETTER OF THE CORRECT ANSWER IN THE SPACE AT THE RIGHT.*

1. According to one suggested filing system, no more than 12 folders should be filed behind any one file guide and from 10 to 20 file guides should be used in each file drawer. Based on this filing system, the MAXIMUM number of folders that a four-drawer file cabinet can hold is

    A. 240   B. 480   C. 960   D. 1,200

2. A certain office uses three different forms. Last year, it used 3,500 copies of Form L, 6,700 copies of Form M, and 10,500 copies of Form P. This year, the office expects to decrease the use of each of these forms by 5%. The TOTAL number of these three forms which the office expects to use this year is

    A. 10,350   B. 16,560   C. 19,665   D. 21,735

3. The hourly rate of pay for a certain part-time employee is computed by dividing his yearly salary rate by the number of hours in the work year. The employee's yearly salary rate is $18,928, and there are 1,820 hours in the work year.
   If this employee works 18 hours during one week, his TOTAL earnings for these 18 hours are

    A. $180.00   B. $183.60   C. $187.20   D. $190.80

4. Assume that the regular work week of an employee is 35 hours and that the employee is paid for any extra hours worked according to the following schedule. For hours worked in excess of 35 hours, up to and including 40 hours, the employee receives his regular hourly rate of pay. For hours worked in excess of 40 hours, the employee receives 1 1/2 times his hourly rate of pay.
   If the employee's hourly rate of pay is $11.20 and he works 43 hours during a certain week, his TOTAL pay for the week would be

    A. $481.60   B. $498.40   C. $556.00   D. $722.40

5. A clerk divided his 35 hour work week as follows:
    1/5 of his time in sorting mail;
    1/2 of his time in filing letters; and
    1/7 of his time in reception work.
   The rest of his time was devoted to messenger work. The percentage of time spent on messenger work by the clerk during the week was MOST NEARLY

    A. 6%   B. 10%   C. 14%   D. 16%

6. A city department has set up a computing unit and has rented 5 computing machines at a yearly rental of $700 per machine. In addition, the cost to the department for the maintenance and repair of each of these machines is $50 per year. Five computing machine operators, each receiving an annual salary of $15,000, and a supervisor, who receives $19,000 a year, have been assigned to this unit. This unit will perform the work previously performed by 10 employees whose combined salary was $162,000 a year.
   On the basis of these facts, the savings that will result from the operation of this computing unit for 5 years will be MOST NEARLY

    A. $250,000   B. $320,000   C. $330,000   D. $475,000

7. Twelve clerks are assigned to enter certain data on index cards. This number of clerks could perform the task in 18 days. After these clerks have worked on this assignment for 6 days, 4 more clerks are added to the staff to do this work.
Assuming that all the clerks work at the same rate of speed, the entire task, instead of taking 18 days, will be performed in _____ days.

   A. 9   B. 12   C. 15   D. 16

8. Suppose that a file cabinet, which has a capacity of 3,000 cards, now contains approximately 2,200 cards. Cards are added to the file at the average rate of 30 cards a day.
To find the number of days it will take to fill the cabinet to capacity,

   A. divide 3,000 by 30
   B. divide 2,200 by 3,000
   C. divide 800 by 30
   D. multiply 30 by the fraction 2,200 divided by 3,000

9. Six gross of special drawing pencils were purchased for use in a city department. If the pencils were used at the rate of 24 a week, the MAXIMUM number of weeks that the six gross of pencils would last is _____ weeks.

   A. 6   B. 12   C. 24   D. 36

10. A stock clerk had 600 pads on hand. He then issued 3/8 of his supply of pads to Division X, 1/4 to Division Y, and 1/6 to Division Z.
The number of pads remaining in stock is

   A. 48   B. 125   C. 240   D. 475

11. If a certain job can be performed by 18 clerks in 26 days, the number of clerks needed to perform the job in 12 days is _____ clerks.

   A. 24   B. 30   C. 39   D. 52

12. In anticipation of a seasonal increase in the amount of work to be performed by his division, a division chief prepared the following list of additional temporary employees needed by his division and the amount of time they would be employed:
   26 cashiers, each at $24,000 a year, for 2 months
   15 laborers, each at $85.00 a day, for 50 days
   6 clerks, each at $21,000 a year, for 3 months
The total approximate cost for this additional personnel would be MOST NEARLY

   A. $200,000   B. $250,000   C. $500,000   D. $600,000

13. A copy machine company offered to sell a city agency 4 copy machines at a discount of 15% from the list price, and to allow the agency $850 for each of its two old machines. The list price of the new machines is $6,250 per machine.
If the city agency accepts this offer, the amount of money it will have to provide for the purchase of these 4 machines is

   A. $17,350   B. $22,950   C. $19,550   D. $18,360

14. A stationery buyer was offered bond paper at the following price scale:
    $1.43 per ream for the first 1,000 reams
    $1.30 per ream for the next 4,000 reams
    $1.20 per ream for each additional ream beyond 5,000 reams
    If the buyer ordered 10,000 reams of paper, the average cost per ream, computed to the nearest cent, was

    A. $1.24 B. $1.26 C. $1.31 D. $1.36

15. A clerk has 5.70 percent of his salary deducted for his retirement pension. If this clerk's annual salary is $20,400, the monthly deduction for his retirement pension is

    A. $298.20 B. $357.90 C. $1,162.80 D. $96.90

16. In a certain bureau, two-thirds of the employees are clerks and the remainder are typists. If there are 90 clerks, then the number of typists in this bureau is

    A. 135 B. 45 C. 120 D. 30

17. The number of investigations conducted by an agency in 1999 was 3,600. In 2000, the number of investigations conducted was one-third more than in 1999. The number of investigations conducted in 2001 was three-fourths of the number conducted in 2000. It is anticipated that the number of investigations conducted in 2002 will be equal to the average of the three preceding years. On the basis of this information, the MOST accurate of the following statements is that the number of investigations conducted in

    A. 1999 is larger than the number anticipated for 2002
    B. 2000 is smaller than the number anticipated for 2002
    C. 2001 is equal to the number conducted in 1999
    D. 2001 is larger than the number anticipated in 2002

18. A city agency engaged in repair work uses a small part which the city purchases for 14¢ each. Assume that, in a certain year, the total expenditure of the city for this part was $700.
    How many of these parts were purchased that year?

    A. 50 B. 200 C. 2,000 D. 5,000

19. The work unit which you supervise is responsible for processing 15 reports per month. If your unit has 4 clerks and the best worker completes 40% of the reports himself, how many reports would each of the other clerks have to complete if they all do an equal number?

    A. 1 B. 2 C. 3 D. 4

20. Assume that the work unit in which you work has 24 clerks and 18 stenographers. In order to change the ratio of stenographers to clerks so that there is 1 stenographer for every 4 clerks, it would be necessary to REDUCE the number of stenographers by

    A. 3   B. 6   C. 9   D. 12

21. The arithmetic mean salary for five employees earning $18,500, $18,300, $18,600, $18,400, and $18,500, respectively, is

    A. $18,450   B. $18,460   C. $18,475   D. $18,500

22. Last year, a city department which is responsible for purchasing supplies ordered bond paper in equal quantities from 22 different companies. The price was exactly the same for each company, and the total cost for the 22 orders was $693,113.
    Assuming prices did not change during the year, the cost of each order was MOST NEARLY

    A. $31,490   B. $31,495   C. $31,500   D. $31,505

23. Suppose that a large bureau has 187 employees. On a particular day, approximately 14% of these employees are not available for work because of absences due to vacation, illness, or other reasons. Of the remaining employees, 1/7 are assigned to a special project while the balance are assigned to the normal work of the bureau. The number of employees assigned to the normal work of the bureau on that day is

    A. 112   B. 124   C. 138   D. 142

24. Suppose that you are in charge of a typing pool of 8 typists. Two typists type at the rate of 38 words per minute; three type at the rate of 40 words per minute; three type at the rate of 42 words per minute. The average typewritten page consists of 50 lines, 12 words per line. Each employee works from 9 to 5 with one hour off for lunch.
    The total number of pages typed by this pool in one day is, on the average, CLOSEST to _____ pages.

    A. 205   B. 225   C. 250   D. 275

25. Suppose that part-time workers are paid $7.20 an hour, prorated to the nearest half hour, with pay guaranteed for a minimum of four hours if services are required for less than four hours. In one operation, part-time workers signed the time sheet as follows:

Worker	In	Out
A	8:00 A.M.	11:35 A.M.
B	8:30 A.M.	3:20 P.M.
C	7:55 A.M.	11:00 A.M.
D	8:30 A.M.	2:25 P.M.

    How much would TOTAL payment to these part-time workers amount to for this operation, assuming that those who stayed after 12 Noon were not paid for one hour which they took off for lunch?

    A. $134.40   B. $136.80   C. $142.20   D. $148.80

KEY (CORRECT ANSWERS)

1.	C	11.	C
2.	C	12.	A
3.	C	13.	C
4.	B	14.	B
5.	D	15.	D
6.	B	16.	B
7.	C	17.	C
8.	C	18.	D
9.	D	19.	C
10.	B	20.	D

21. B
22. D
23. C
24. B
25. B

SOLUTIONS TO PROBLEMS

1. Maximum number of folders = (4)(12)(20) = 960

2. (3500+6700+10,500)(.95) = 19,665

3. Hourly rate = $18,928 ÷ 1820 = $10.40. Then, the pay for 18 hours = ($10.40)(18) = $187.20

4. Total pay = ($11.20)(40) + ($11.20)(1.5)(3) = $498.40

5. (1 - 1/5 - 1/2 - 1/7)(100)% ≈ 16%

6. Previous cost for five years = ($324,000)(5) = $1,620,000
   Present cost for five years = (5)(5)($1,400) + (5)(5)($100) + (5)(5)($30,000) + (1)(5)($38,000) = $977,500   The net savings = $642,500 ≈ $640,000

7. (12)(18) = 216 clerk-days. Then, 216 - (12)(6) = 144 clerk-days of work left when 4 more clerks are added. Now, 16 clerks will finish the task in 144 ÷ 16 = 9 more days. Finally, the task will require a total of 6 + 9 = 15 days.

8. Number of days needed = (3000-2200) ÷ 30 = 26.7, which is equivalent to dividing 800 by 30.

9. (6)(144) = 864 pencils purchased. Then, 864 ÷ 24 = 36 maximum number of weeks

10. Number of remaining pads = 600 - (1)(600) - (1/4)(600) - (1/6)(600) = 125

11. (18)(26) ÷ 12 = 39 clerks

12. Total cost = (26)($24,000)(2/12) + (15)($85)(50) + (6)($21,000)(3/12) = $199,250 $200,000

13. (4)($6250)(.85) - (2)($850) = $19,550

14. Total cost = ($1.43)(1000) + ($1.30)(4000) + ($1.20X5000) = $12,630. Average cost per ream = $12,630 10,000 ≈ $1.26

15. Monthly salary = $20,400 ÷ 12 = $1700. Thus, the monthly deduction for his pension = ($1700)(.057) + $96.90

16. Number of employees = 90 ÷ 2/3 = 135. Then, the number of typists = (1/3)(135) = 45

17. The number of investigations for each year is as follows:
    1999: 3600
    2000: (3600)(1 1/3) = 4800
    2001: (4800)(3/4) = 3600
    2002: (3600+4800+3600)/3 = 4000
    So, the number of investigations were equal for 1999 and 2001.

18. $700 ÷ .14 = 5000 parts

19. The best worker does (.40)(15) = 6 reports. The other 9 reports are divided equally among the other 3 clerks, so each clerk does 9 ÷ 3 = 3 reports.

20. 1:4 = 6:24 . Thus, the number of stenographers must be reduced by 18 - 6 = 12

21. Mean = ($18,500+$18,300+$18,400+$18,500) ÷ 5 = $18,460

22. The cost per order = $693,113 ÷ 22 ≈ $31,505

23. 187 - (.14) = 26. 187 - 26 = 161 - 1/7 (161) = 23
    161 - 23 = 138

24. Number of words typed in 1 min. = (2)(38) + (3)(40) + (3)(42) = 322. For 7 hours, the total number of words typed = (7)(60)(322) = 135,240. Each page contains (on the average) (50)(12) = 600 words. Finally, 135,240 ÷ 600 ≈ 225 pages

25. Worker A = ($7.20)(4) = $28.80
    Worker B = ($7.20)(3 1/2) + ($7.20)(2 1/2) = $43.20
    Worker C = ($7.20)(4) = $28.80
    Worker D = ($7.20)(3 1/2) + ($7.20)(1 1/2) = $36.00
    Total for all 4 workers = $136.80
    Note: Workers A and C received the guaranteed minimum 4 hours pay each.

PHILOSOPHY, PRINCIPLES, PRACTICES, AND TECHNICS
OF
SUPERVISION, ADMINISTRATION, MANAGEMENT, AND ORGANIZATION

TABLE OF CONTENTS

	Page
MEANING OF SUPERVISION	1
THE OLD AND THE NEW SUPERVISION	1
THE EIGHT (8) BASIC PRINCIPLES OF THE NEW SUPERVISION	1
I. Principle of Responsibility	1
II. Principle of Authority	2
III. Principle of Self-Growth	2
IV. Principle of Individual Worth	2
V. Principle of Creative Leadership	2
VI. Principle of Success and Failure	2
VII. Principle of Science	3
VIII. Principle of Cooperation	3
WHAT IS ADMINISTRATION?	3
I. Practices Commonly Classed as "Supervisory"	3
II. Practices Commonly Classed as "Administrative"	3
III. Practices Commonly Classed as Both "Supervisory" and "Administrative"	4
RESPONSIBILITIES OF THE SUPERVISOR	4
COMPETENCIES OF THE SUPERVISOR	4
THE PROFESSIONAL SUPERVISOR-EMPLOYEE RELATIONSHIP	4
MINI-TEXT IN SUPERVISION, ADMINISTRATION, MANAGEMENT, AND ORGANIZATION	5
I. Brief Highlights	5
A. Levels of Management	6
B. What the Supervisor Must Learn	6
C. A Definition of Supervision	6
D. Elements of the Team Concept	6
E. Principles of Organization	6
F. The Four Important Parts of Every Job	7
G. Principles of Delegation	7
H. Principles of Effective Communications	7
I. Principles of Work Improvement	7
J. Areas of Job Improvement	7
K. Seven Key Points in Making Improvements	8

L.	Corrective Techniques for Job Improvement	8
M.	A Planning Checklist	8
N.	Five Characteristics of Good Directions	9
O.	Types of Directions	9
P.	Controls	9
Q.	Orienting the New Employee	9
R.	Checklist for Orienting New Employees	9
S.	Principles of Learning	10
T.	Causes of Poor Performance	10
U.	Four Major Steps in On-the-Job Instructions	10
V.	Employees Want Five Things	10
W.	Some Don'ts in Regard to Praise	11
X.	How to Gain Your Workers' Confidence	11
Y.	Sources of Employee Problems	11
Z.	The Supervisor's Key to Discipline	11
AA.	Five Important Processes of Management	12
BB.	When the Supervisor Fails to Plan	12
CC.	Fourteen General Principles of Management	12
DD.	Change	12

II. Brief Topical Summaries — 13
    A. Who/What is the Supervisor? — 13
    B. The Sociology of Work — 13
    C. Principles and Practices of Supervision — 14
    D. Dynamic Leadership — 14
    E. Processes for Solving Problems — 15
    F. Training for Results — 15
    G. Health, Safety, and Accident Prevention — 16
    H. Equal Employment Opportunity — 16
    I. Improving Communications — 16
    J. Self-Development — 17
    K. Teaching and Training — 17
        1. The Teaching Process — 17
            a. Preparation — 17
            b. Presentation — 18
            c. Summary — 18
            d. Application — 18
            e. Evaluation — 18
        2. Teaching Methods — 18
            a. Lecture — 18
            b. Discussion — 18
            c. Demonstration — 19
            d. Performance — 19
            e. Which Method to Use — 19

PHILOSOPHY, PRINCIPLES, PRACTICES, AND TECHNICS
OF
SUPERVISION, ADMINISTRATION, MANAGEMENT, AND ORGANIZATION

MEANING OF SUPERVISION

The extension of the democratic philosophy has been accompanied by an extension in the scope of supervision. Modern leaders and supervisors no longer think of supervision in the narrow sense of being confined chiefly to visiting employees, supplying materials, or rating the staff. They regard supervision as being intimately related to all the concerned agencies of society, they speak of the supervisor's function in terms of "growth," rather than the "improvement" of employees.

This modern concept of supervision may be defined as follows: Supervision is leadership and the development of leadership within groups which are cooperatively engaged in inspection, research, training, guidance, and evaluation.

THE OLD AND THE NEW SUPERVISION

TRADITIONAL
1. Inspection
2. Focused on the employee
3. Visitation
4. Random and haphazard
5. Imposed and authoritarian
6. One person usually

MODERN
1. Study and analysis
2. Focused on aims, materials, methods, supervisors, employees, environment
3. Demonstrations, intervisitation, workshops, directed reading, bulletins, etc.
4. Definitely organized and planned (scientific)
5. Cooperative and democratic
6. Many persons involved (creative)

THE EIGHT (8) BASIC PRINCIPLES OF THE NEW SUPERVISION

I. Principle of Responsibility
   Authority to act and responsibility for acting must be joined.
   A. If you give responsibility, give authority.
   B. Define employee duties clearly.
   C. Protect employees from criticism by others.
   D. Recognize the rights as well as obligations of employees.
   E. Achieve the aims of a democratic society insofar as it is possible within the area of your work.
   F. Establish a situation favorable to training and learning.
   G. Accept ultimate responsibility for everything done in your section, unit, office, division, department.
   H. Good administration and good supervision are inseparable.

II. Principle of Authority
   The success of the supervisor is measured by the extent to which the power of authority is not used.
   A. Exercise simplicity and informality in supervision
   B. Use the simplest machinery of supervision
   C. If it is good for the organization as a whole, it is probably justified.
   D. Seldom be arbitrary or authoritative.
   E. Do not base your work on the power of position or of personality.
   F. Permit and encourage the free expression of opinions.

III. Principle of Self-Growth
   The success of the supervisor is measured by the extent to which, and the speed with which, he is no longer needed.
   A. Base criticism on principles, not on specifics.
   B. Point out higher activities to employees.
   C. Train for self-thinking by employees to meet new situations.
   D. Stimulate initiative, self-reliance, and individual responsibility
   E. Concentrate on stimulating the growth of employees rather than on removing defects.

IV. Principle of Individual Worth
   Respect for the individual is a paramount consideration in supervision.
   A. Be human and sympathetic in dealing with employees.
   B. Don't nag about things to be done.
   C. Recognize the individual differences among employees and seek opportunities to permit best expression of each personality.

V. Principle of Creative Leadership
   The best supervision is that which is not apparent to the employee.
   A. Stimulate, don't drive employees to creative action.
   B. Emphasize doing good things.
   C. Encourage employees to do what they do best.
   D. Do not be too greatly concerned with details of subject or method.
   E. Do not be concerned exclusively with immediate problems and activities.
   F. Reveal higher activities and make them both desired and maximally possible.
   G. Determine procedures in the light of each situation but see that these are derived from a sound basic philosophy.
   H. Aid, inspire, and lead so as to liberate the creative spirit latent in all good employees.

VI. Principle of Success and Failure
   There are no unsuccessful employees, only unsuccessful supervisors who have failed to give proper leadership.
   A. Adapt suggestions to the capacities, attitudes, and prejudices of employees.
   B. Be gradual, be progressive, be persistent.
   C. Help the employee find the general principle; have the employee apply his own problem to the general principle.
   D. Give adequate appreciation for good work and honest effort.
   E. Anticipate employee difficulties and help to prevent them.
   F. Encourage employees to do the desirable things they will do anyway.
   G. Judge your supervision by the results it secures.

VII. Principle of Science
Successful supervision is scientific, objective, and experimental. It is based on facts, not on prejudices.
   A. Be cumulative in results.
   B. Never divorce your suggestions from the goals of training.
   C. Don't be impatient of results.
   D. Keep all matters on a professional, not a personal, level.
   E. Do not be concerned exclusively with immediate problems and activities.
   F. Use objective means of determining achievement and rating where possible.

VIII. Principle of Cooperation
Supervision is a cooperative enterprise between supervisor and employee.
   A. Begin with conditions as they are.
   B. Ask opinions of all involved when formulating policies.
   C. Organization is as good as its weakest link.
   D. Let employees help to determine policies and department programs.
   E. Be approachable and accessible—physically and mentally.
   F. Develop pleasant social relationships.

WHAT IS ADMINISTRATION

Administration is concerned with providing the environment, the material facilities, and the operational procedures that will promote the maximum growth and development of supervisors and employees. (Organization is an aspect and a concomitant of administration.)

There is no sharp line of demarcation between supervision and administration; these functions are intimately interrelated and, often, overlapping. They are complementary activities.

I. Practices Commonly Classed as "Supervisory"
   A. Conducting employees' conferences
   B. Visiting sections, units, offices, divisions, departments
   C. Arranging for demonstrations
   D. Examining plans
   E. Suggesting professional reading
   F. Interpreting bulletins
   G. Recommending in-service training courses
   H. Encouraging experimentation
   I. Appraising employee morale
   J. Providing for intervisitation

II. Practices Commonly Classified as "Administrative"
   A. Management of the office
   B. Arrangement of schedules for extra duties
   C. Assignment of rooms or areas
   D. Distribution of supplies
   E. Keeping records and reports
   F. Care of audio-visual materials
   G. Keeping inventory records
   H. Checking record cards and books

    I.   Programming special activities
    J.   Checking on the attendance and punctuality of employees

III.   Practices Commonly Classified as Both "Supervisory" and "Administrative"
    A.   Program construction
    B.   Testing or evaluating outcomes
    C.   Personnel accounting
    D.   Ordering instructional materials

RESPONSIBILITIES OF THE SUPERVISOR

A person employed in a supervisory capacity must constantly be able to improve his own efficiency and ability. He represent the employer to the employees and only continuous self-examination can make him a capable supervisor.

Leadership and training are the supervisor's responsibility. An efficient working unit is one in which the employees work with the supervisor. It is his job to bring out the best in his employees. He must always be relaxed, courteous, and calm in his association with his employees. Their feelings are important, and a harsh attitude does not develop the most efficient employees.

COMPETENCES OF THE SUPERVISOR

I.   Complete knowledge of the duties and responsibilities of his position.
II.   To be able to organize a job, plan ahead, and carry through.
III.   To have self-confidence and initiative.
IV.   To be able to handle the unexpected situation and make quick decisions.
V.   To be able to properly train subordinates in the positions they are best suited for.
VI.   To be able to keep good human relations among his subordinates.
VII.   To be able to keep good human relations between his subordinates and himself and to earn their respect and trust.

THE PROFESSIONAL SUPERVISOR-EMPLOYEE RELATIONSHIP

There are two kinds of efficiency: one kind is only apparent and is produced in organizations through the exercise of mere discipline; this is but a simulation of the second, or true, efficiency which springs from spontaneous cooperation. If you are a manager, no matter how great or small your responsibility, it is your job, in the final analysis, to create and develop this involuntary cooperation among the people whom you supervise. For, no matter how powerful a combination of money, machines, and materials a company may have, this is a dead and sterile thing without a team of willing, thinking, and articulate people to guide it.

The following 21 points are presented as indicative of the exemplary basic relationship that should exist between supervisor and employee:

1. Each person wants to be liked and respected by his fellow employee and wants to be treated with consideration and respect by his superior.
2. The most competent employee will make an error. However, in a unit where good relations exist between the supervisor and his employees, tenseness and fear do not exist. Thus, errors are not hidden or covered up, and the efficiency of a unit is not impaired.

3. Subordinates resent rules, regulations, or orders that are unreasonable or unexplained.
4. Subordinates are quick to resent unfairness, harshness, injustices, and favoritism.
5. An employee will accept responsibility if he knows that he will be complimented for a job well done, and not too harshly chastised for failure; that his supervisor will check the cause of the failure, and, if it was the supervisor's fault, he will assume the blame therefore. If it was the employee's fault, his supervisor will explain the correct method or means of handling the responsibility.
6. An employee wants to receive credit for a suggestion he has made, that is used. If a suggestion cannot be used, the employee is entitled to an explanation. The supervisor should not say "no" and close the subject.
7. Fear and worry slow up a worker's ability. Poor working environment can impair his physical and mental health. A good supervisor avoids forceful methods, threats, and arguments to get a job done.
8. A forceful supervisor is able to train his employees individually and as a team, and is able to motivate them in the proper channels.
9. A mature supervisor is able to properly evaluate his subordinates and to keep them happy and satisfied.
10. A sensitive supervisor will never patronize his subordinates.
11. A worthy supervisor will respect his employees' confidences.
12. Definite and clear-cut responsibilities should be assigned to each executive.
13. Responsibility should always be coupled with corresponding authority.
14. No change should be made in the scope or responsibilities of a position without a definite understanding to that effect on the part of all persons concerned.
15. No executive or employee, occupying a single position in the organization, should be subject to definite orders from more than one source.
16. Orders should never be given to subordinates over the head of a responsible executive. Rather than do this, the officer in question should be supplanted.
17. Criticisms of subordinates should, whoever possible, be made privately, and in no case should a subordinate be criticized in the presence of executives or employees of equal or lower rank.
18. No dispute or difference between executives or employees as to authority or responsibilities should be considered too trivial for prompt and careful adjudication.
19. Promotions, wage changes, and disciplinary action should always be approved by the executive immediately superior to the one directly responsible.
20. No executive or employee should ever be required, or expected, to be at the same time an assistant to, and critic of, another.
21. Any executive whose work is subject to regular inspection should, wherever practicable, be given the assistance and facilities necessary to enable him to maintain an independent check of the quality of his work.

MINI-TEXT IN SUPERVISION, ADMINISTRATION, MANAGEMENT, AND ORGANIZATION

I. Brief Highlights

Listed concisely and sequentially are major headings and important data in the field for quick recall and review.

A. Levels of Management
Any organization of some size has several levels of management. In terms of a ladder, the levels are:

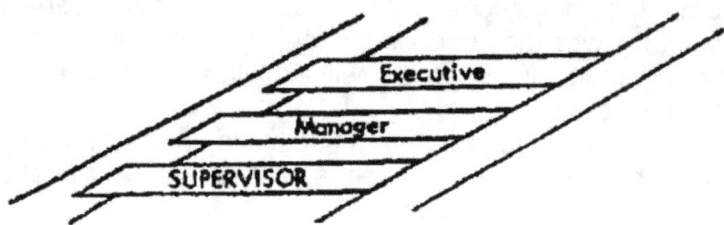

The first level is very important because it is the beginning point of management leadership.

B. What the Supervisor Must Learn
A supervisor must learn to:
1. Deal with people and their differences
2. Get the job done through people
3. Recognize the problems when they exist
4. Overcome obstacles to good performance
5. Evaluate the performance of people
6. Check his own performance in terms of accomplishment

C. A Definition of Supervisor
The term supervisor means any individual having authority, in the interests of the employer, to hire, transfer, suspend, lay-off, recall, promote, discharge, assign, reward, or discipline other employees or responsibility to direct them, or to adjust their grievances, or effectively to recommend such action, if, in connection with the foregoing, exercise of such authority is not of a merely routine or clerical nature but requires the use of independent judgment.

D. Elements of the Team Concept
What is involved in teamwork? The component parts are:
1. Members
2. A leader
3. Goals
4. Plans
5. Cooperation
6. Spirit

E. Principles of Organization
1. A team member must know what his job is.
2. Be sure that the nature and scope of a job are understood.
3. Authority and responsibility should be carefully spelled out.
4. A supervisor should be permitted to make the maximum number of decisions affecting his employees.
5. Employees should report to only one supervisor.
6. A supervisor should direct only as many employees as he can handle effectively.
7. An organization plan should be flexible.

8. Inspection and performance of work should be separate.
9. Organizational problems should receive immediate attention.
10. Assign work in line with ability and experience.

F. The Four Important Parts of Every Job
1. Inherent in every job is the *accountability* for results.
2. A second set of factors in every job is *responsibilities*.
3. Along with duties and responsibilities one must have the *authority* to act within certain limits without obtaining permission to proceed.
4. No job exists in a vacuum. The supervisor is surrounded by key *relationships*.

G. Principles of Delegation
Where work is delegated for the first time, the supervisor should think in terms of these questions:
1. Who is best qualified to do this?
2. Can an employee improve his abilities by doing this?
3. How long should an employee spend on this?
4. Are there any special problems for which he will need guidance?
5. How broad a delegation can I make?

H. Principles of Effective Communications
1. Determine the media.
2. To whom directed?
3. Identification and source authority.
4. Is communication understood?

I. Principles of Work Improvement
1. Most people usually do only the work which is assigned to them.
2. Workers are likely to fit assigned work into the time available to perform it.
3. A good workload usually stimulates output.
4. People usually do their best work when they know that results will be reviewed or inspected.
5. Employees usually feel that someone else is responsible for conditions of work, workplace layout, job methods, type of tools/equipment, and other such factors.
6. Employees are usually defensive about their job security.
7. Employees have natural resistance to change.
8. Employees can support or destroy a supervisor.
9. A supervisor usually earns the respect of his people through his personal example of diligence and efficiency.

J. Areas of Job Improvement
The areas of job improvement are quite numerous, but the most common ones which a supervisor can identify and utilize are:
1. Departmental layout
2. Flow of work
3. Workplace layout
4. Utilization of manpower
5. Work methods
6. Materials handling

7. Utilization
8. Motion economy

K. Seven Key Points in Making Improvements
1. Select the job to be improved
2. Study how it is being done now
3. Question the present method
4. Determine actions to be taken
5. Chart proposed method
6. Get approval and apply
7. Solicit worker participation

L. Corrective Techniques of Job Improvement
Specific Problems
1. Size of workload
2. Inability to meet schedules
3. Strain and fatigue
4. Improper use of men and skills
5. Waste, poor quality, unsafe conditions
6. Bottleneck conditions that hinder output
7. Poor utilization of equipment and machine
8. Efficiency and productivity of labor

General Improvement
1. Departmental layout
2. Flow of work
3. Work plan layout
4. Utilization of manpower
5. Work methods
6. Materials handling
7. Utilization of equipment
8. Motion economy

Corrective Techniques
1. Study with scale model
2. Flow chart study
3. Motion analysis
4. Comparison of units produced to standard allowance
5. Methods analysis
6. Flow chart and equipment study
7. Down time vs. running time
8. Motion analysis

M. A Planning Checklist
1. Objectives
2. Controls
3. Delegations
4. Communications
5. Resources
6. Manpower

7. Equipment
8. Supplies and materials
9. Utilization of time
10. Safety
11. Money
12. Work
13. Timing of improvements

N. Five Characteristics of Good Directions
In order to get results, directions must be:
1. Possible of accomplishment
2. Agreeable with worker interests
3. Related to mission
4. Planned and complete
5. Unmistakably clear

O. Types of Directions
1. Demands or direct orders
2. Requests
3. Suggestion or implication
4. volunteering

P. Controls
A typical listing of the overall areas in which the supervisor should establish controls might be:
1. Manpower
2. Materials
3. Quality of work
4. Quantity of work
5. Time
6. Space
7. Money
8. Methods

Q. Orienting the New Employee
1. Prepare for him
2. Welcome the new employee
3. Orientation for the job
4. Follow-up

R. Checklist for Orienting New Employees

		Yes	No
1.	Do you appreciate the feelings of new employees when they first report for work?	___	___
2.	Are you aware of the fact that the new employee must make a big adjustment to his job?	___	___
3.	Have you given him good reasons for liking the job and the organization?	___	___
4.	Have you prepared for his first day on the job?	___	___
5.	Did you welcome him cordially and make him feel needed?	___	___

                                                                    Yes   No

    6. Did you establish rapport with him so that he feels free to talk and discuss matters with you?

    7. Did you explain his job to him and his relationship to you?

    8. Does he know that his work will be evaluated periodically on a basis that is fair and objective?

    9. Did you introduce him to his fellow workers in such a way that they are likely to accept him?

    10. Does he know what employee benefits he will receive?

    11. Does he understand the importance of being on the job and what to do if he must leave his duty station?

    12. Has he been impressed with the importance of accident prevention and safe practice?

    13. Does he generally know his way around the department?

    14. Is he under the guidance of a sponsor who will teach the right way of doing things?

    15. Do you plan to follow-up so that he will continue to adjust successfully to his job?

S. Principles of Learning
1. Motivation
2. Demonstration or explanation
3. Practice

T. Causes of Poor Performance
1. Improper training for job
2. Wrong tools
3. Inadequate directions
4. Lack of supervisory follow-up
5. Poor communications
6. Lack of standards of performance
7. Wrong work habits
8. Low morale
9. Other

U. Four Major Steps in On-The-Job Instruction
1. Prepare the worker
2. Present the operation
3. Tryout performance
4. Follow-up

V. Employees Want Five Things
1. Security
2. Opportunity
3. Recognition
4. Inclusion
5. Expression

W. Some Don'ts in Regard to Praise
1. Don't praise a person for something he hasn't done.
2. Don't praise a person unless you can be sincere.
3. Don't be sparing in praise just because your superior withholds it from you.
4. Don't let too much time elapse between good performance and recognition of it

X. How to Gain Your Workers' Confidence
Methods of developing confidence include such things as:
1. Knowing the interests, habits, hobbies of employees
2. Admitting your own inadequacies
3. Sharing and telling of confidence in others
4. Supporting people when they are in trouble
5. Delegating matters that can be well handled
6. Being frank and straightforward about problems and working conditions
7. Encouraging others to bring their problems to you
8. Taking action on problems which impede worker progress

Y. Sources of Employee Problems
On-the-job causes might be such things as:
1. A feeling that favoritism is exercised in assignments
2. Assignment of overtime
3. An undue amount of supervision
4. Changing methods or systems
5. Stealing of ideas or trade secrets
6. Lack of interest in job
7. Threat of reduction in force
8. Ignorance or lack of communications
9. Poor equipment
10. Lack of knowing how supervisor feels toward employee
11. Shift assignments

Off-the-job problems might have to do with:
1. Health
2. Finances
3. Housing
4. Family

Z. The Supervisor's Key to Discipline
There are several key points about discipline which the supervisor should keep in mind:
1. Job discipline is one of the disciplines of life and is directed by the supervisor.
2. It is more important to correct an employee fault than to fix blame for it.
3. Employee performance is affected by problems both on the job and off.
4. Sudden or abrupt changes in behavior can be indications of important employee problems.
5. Problems should be dealt with as soon as possible after they are identified.
6. The attitude of the supervisor may have more to do with solving problems than the techniques of problem solving.
7. Correction of employee behavior should be resorted to only after the supervisor is sure that training or counseling will not be helpful.

8. Be sure to document your disciplinary actions.
9. Make sure that you are disciplining on the basis of facts rather than personal feelings.
10. Take each disciplinary step in order, being careful not to make snap judgments, or decisions based on impatience.

AA. Five Important Processes of Management
1. Planning
2. Organizing
3. Scheduling
4. Controlling
5. Motivating

BB. When the Supervisor Fails to Plan
1. Supervisor creates impression of not knowing his job
2. May lead to excessive overtime
3. Job runs itself—supervisor lacks control
4. Deadlines and appointments missed
5. Parts of the work go undone
6. Work interrupted by emergencies
7. Sets a bad example
8. Uneven workload creates peaks and valleys
9. Too much time on minor details at expense of more important tasks

CC. Fourteen General Principles of Management
1. Division of work
2. Authority and responsibility
3. Discipline
4. Unity of command
5. Unity of direction
6. Subordination of individual interest to general interest
7. Remuneration of personnel
8. Centralization
9. Scalar chain
10. Order
11. Equity
12. Stability of tenure of personnel
13. Initiative
14. Esprit de corps

DD. Change

Bringing about change is perhaps attempted more often, and yet less well understood, than anything else the supervisor does. How do people generally react to change? (People tend to resist change that is imposed upon them by other individuals or circumstances.

Change is characteristic of every situation. It is a part of every real endeavor where the efforts of people are concerned.

1. Why do people resist change?
   People may resist change because of:
   a. Fear of the unknown
   b. Implied criticism
   c. Unpleasant experiences in the past
   d. Fear of loss of status
   e. Threat to the ego
   f. Fear of loss of economic stability

2. How can we best overcome the resistance to change?
   In initiating change, take these steps:
   a. Get ready to sell
   b. Identify sources of help
   c. Anticipate objections
   d. Sell benefits
   e. Listen in depth
   f. Follow up

II. Brief Topical Summaries

   A. Who/What is the Supervisor?
      1. The supervisor is often called the "highest level employee and the lowest level manager."
      2. A supervisor is a member of both management and the work group. He acts as a bridge between the two.
      3. Most problems in supervision are in the area of human relations, or people problems.
      4. Employees expect: Respect, opportunity to learn and to advance, and a sense of belonging, and so forth.
      5. Supervisors are responsible for directing people and organizing work. Planning is of paramount importance.
      6. A position description is a set of duties and responsibilities inherent to a given position.
      7. It is important to keep the position description up-to-date and to provide each employee with his own copy.

   B. The Sociology of Work
      1. People are alike in many ways; however, each individual is unique.
      2. The supervisor is challenged in getting to know employee differences. Acquiring skills in evaluating individuals is an asset.
      3. Maintaining meaningful working relationships in the organization is of great importance.
      4. The supervisor has an obligation to help individuals to develop to their fullest potential.
      5. Job rotation on a planned basis helps to build versatility and to maintain interest and enthusiasm in work groups.
      6. Cross training (job rotation) provides backup skills.

7. The supervisor can help reduce tension by maintaining a sense of humor, providing guidance to employees, and by making reasonable and timely decisions. Employees respond favorably to working under reasonably predictable circumstances.
8. Change is characteristic of all managerial behavior. The supervisor must adjust to changes in procedures, new methods, technological changes, and to a number of new and sometimes challenging situations.
9. To overcome the natural tendency for people to resist change, the supervisor should become more skillful in initiating change.

C. Principles and Practices of Supervision
1. Employees should be required to answer to only one superior.
2. A supervisor can effectively direct only a limited number of employees, depending upon the complexity, variety, and proximity of the jobs involved.
3. The organizational chart presents the organization in graphic form. It reflects lines of authority and responsibility as well as interrelationships of units within the organization.
4. Distribution of work can be improved through an analysis using the "Work Distribution Chart."
5. The "Work Distribution Chart" reflects the division of work within a unit in understandable form.
6. When related tasks are given to an employee, he has a better chance of increasing his skills through training.
7. The individual who is given the responsibility for tasks must also be given the appropriate authority to insure adequate results.
8. The supervisor should delegate repetitive, routine work. Preparation of recurring reports, maintaining leave and attendance records are some examples.
9. Good discipline is essential to good task performance. Discipline is reflected in the actions of employees on the job in the absence of supervision.
10. Disciplinary action may have to be taken when the positive aspects of discipline have failed. Reprimand, warning, and suspension are examples of disciplinary action.
11. If a situation calls for a reprimand, be sure it is deserved and remember it is to be done in private.

D. Dynamic Leadership
1. A style is a personal method or manner of exerting influence.
2. Authoritarian leaders often see themselves as the source of power and authority.
3. The democratic leader often perceives the group as the source of authority and power.
4. Supervisors tend to do better when using the pattern of leadership that is most natural for them.
5. Social scientists suggest that the effective supervisor use the leadership style that best fits the problem or circumstances involved.
6. All four styles—telling, selling, consulting, joining—have their place. Using one does not preclude using the other at another time.

7. The theory X point of view assumes that the average person dislikes work, will avoid it whenever possible, and must be coerced to achieve organizational objectives.
8. The theory Y point of view assumes that the average person considers work to be a natural as play, and, when the individual is committed, he requires little supervision or direction to accomplish desired objectives.
9. The leader's basic assumptions concerning human behavior and human nature affect his actions, decisions, and other managerial practices.
10. Dissatisfaction among employees is often present, but difficult to isolate. The supervisor should seek to weaken dissatisfaction by keeping promises, being sincere and considerate, keeping employees informed, and so forth.
11. Constructive suggestions should be encouraged during the natural progress of the work.

E. Processes for Solving Problems
1. People find their daily tasks more meaningful and satisfying when they can improve them.
2. The causes of problems, or the key factors, are often hidden in the background. Ability to solve problems often involves the ability to isolate them from their backgrounds. There is some substance to the cliché that some persons "can't see the forest for the trees."
3. New procedures are often developed from old ones. Problems should be broken down into manageable parts. New ideas can be adapted from old one.
4. People think differently in problem-solving situations. Using a logical, patterned approach is often useful. One approach found to be useful includes these steps:
   a. Define the problem
   b. Establish objectives
   c. Get the facts
   d. Weigh and decide
   e. Take action
   f. Evaluate action

F. Training for Results
1. Participants respond best when they feel training is important to them.
2. The supervisor has responsibility for the training and development of those who report to him.
3. When training is delegated to others, great care must be exercised to insure the trainer has knowledge, aptitude, and interest for his work as a trainer.
4. Training (learning) of some type goes on continually. The most successful supervisor makes certain the learning contributes in a productive manner to operational goals.
5. New employees are particularly susceptible to training. Older employees facing new job situations require specific training, as well as having need for development and growth opportunities.
6. Training needs require continuous monitoring.
7. The training officer of an agency is a professional with a responsibility to assist supervisors in solving training problems.

8. Many of the self-development steps important to the supervisor's own growth are equally important to the development of peers and subordinates. Knowledge of these is important when the supervisor consults with others on development and growth opportunities.

G. Health, Safety, and Accident Prevention
1. Management-minded supervisors take appropriate measures to assist employees in maintaining health and in assuring safe practices in the work environment.
2. Effective safety training and practices help to avoid injury and accidents.
3. Safety should be a management goal. All infractions of safety which are observed should be corrected without exception.
4. Employees' safety attitude, training and instruction, provision of safe tools and equipment, supervision, and leadership are considered highly important factors which contribute to safety and which can be influenced directly by supervisors.
5. When accidents do occur, they should be investigated promptly for very important reasons, including the fact that information which is gained can be used to prevent accidents in the future.

H. Equal Employment Opportunity
1. The supervisor should endeavor to treat all employees fairly, without regard to religion, race, sex, or national origin.
2. Groups tend to reflect the attitude of the leader. Prejudice can be detected even in very subtle form. Supervisors must strive to create a feeling of mutual respect and confidence in every employee.
3. Complete utilization of all human resources is a national goal. Equitable consideration should be accorded women in the work force, minority-group members, the physically and mentally handicapped, and the older employee. The important question is: "Who can do the job?"
4. Training opportunities, recognition for performance, overtime assignments, promotional opportunities, and all other personnel actions are to be handled on an equitable basis.

I. Improving Communications
1. Communications is achieving understanding between the sender and the receiver of a message. It also means sharing information—the creation of understanding.
2. Communication is basic to all human activity. Words are means of conveying meanings; however, real meanings are in people.
3. There are very practical differences in the effectiveness of one-way, impersonal, and two-way communications. Words spoken face-to-face are better understood. Telephone conversations are effective, but lack the rapport of person-to-person exchanges. The whole person communicates.
4. Cooperation and communication in an organization go hand in hand. When there is a mutual respect between people, spelling out rules and procedures for communicating is unnecessary.
5. There are several barriers to effective communications. These include failure to listen with respect and understanding, lack of skill in feedback, and misinterpreting the meanings of words used by the speaker. It is also common

practice to listen to what we want to hear, and tune out things we do not want to hear.
6. Communication is management's chief problem. The supervisor should accept the challenge to communicate more effectively and to improve interagency and intra-agency communications.
7. The supervisor may often plan for and conduct meetings. The planning phase is critical and may determine the success or the failure of a meeting.
8. Speaking before groups usually requires extra effort. Stage fright may never disappear completely, but it can be controlled.

J. Self-Development
1. Every employee is responsible for his own self-development.
2. Toastmaster and toastmistress clubs offer opportunities to improve skills in oral communications.
3. Planning for one's own self-development is of vital importance. Supervisors know their own strengths and limitations better than anyone else.
4. Many opportunities are open to aid the supervisor in his developmental efforts, including job assignments; training opportunities, both governmental and non-governmental—to include universities and professional conferences and seminars.
5. Programmed instruction offers a means of studying at one's own rate.
6. Where difficulties may arise from a supervisor's being away from his work for training, he may participate in televised home study or correspondence courses to meet his self-development needs.

K. Teaching and Training
1. The Teaching Process
Teaching is encouraging and guiding the learning activities of students toward established goals. In most cases this process consists of five steps: preparation, presentation, summarization, evaluation, and application.

   a. Preparation
   Preparation is two-fold in nature; that of the supervisor and the employee. Preparation by the supervisor is absolutely essential to success. He must know what, when, where, how, and whom he will teach. Some of the factors that should be considered are:
   1) The objectives
   2) The materials needed
   3) The methods to be used
   4) Employee participation
   5) Employee interest
   6) Training aids
   7) Evaluation
   8) Summarization

   Employee preparation consists in preparing the employee to receive the material. Probably the most important single factor in the preparation of the employee is arousing and maintaining his interest. He must know the objectives of the training, why he is there, how the material can be used, and its importance to him.

b. Presentation
   In presentation, have a carefully designed plan and follow it. The plan should be accurate and complete, yet flexible enough to meet situations as they arise. The method of presentation will be determined by the particular situation and objectives.

c. Summary
   A summary should be made at the end of every training unit and program. In addition, there may be internal summaries depending on the nature of the material being taught. The important thing is that the trainee must always be able to understand how each part of the new material relates to the whole.

d. Application
   The supervisor must arrange work so the employee will be given a chance to apply new knowledge or skills while the material is still clear in his mind and interest is high. The trainee does not really know whether he has learned the material until he has been given a chance to apply it. If the material is not applied, it loses most of its value.

e. Evaluation
   The purpose of all training is to promote learning. To determine whether the training has been a success or failure, the supervisor must evaluate this learning.
   In the broadest sense, evaluation includes all the devices, methods, skills, and techniques used by the supervisor to keep himself and the employees informed as to their progress toward the objectives they are pursuing. The extent to which the employee has mastered the knowledge, skills, and abilities, or changed his attitudes, as determined by the program objectives, is the extent to which instruction has succeeded or failed.
   Evaluation should not be confined to the end of the lesson, day, or program but should be used continuously. We shall note later the way this relates to the rest of the teaching process.

2. Teaching Methods
   A teaching method is a pattern of identifiable student and instructor activity used in presenting training material.
   All supervisors are faced with the problem of deciding which method should be used at a given time.

   a. Lecture
      The lecture is direct oral presentation of material by the supervisor. The present trend is to place less emphasis on the trainer's activity and more on that of the trainee.

   b. Discussion
      Teaching by discussion or conference involves using questions and other techniques to arouse interest and focus attention upon certain areas, and by doing so creating a learning situation. This can be one of the most

valuable methods because it gives the employees an opportunity to express their ideas and pool their knowledge.

    c. Demonstration
The demonstration is used to teach how something works or how to do something. It can be used to show a principle or what the results of a series of actions will be. A well-staged demonstration is particularly effective because it shows proper methods of performance in a realistic manner.

    d. Performance
Performance is one of the most fundamental of all learning techniques or teaching methods. The trainee may be able to tell how a specific operation should be performed but he cannot be sure he knows how to perform the operation until he has done so.
As with all methods, there are certain advantages and disadvantages to each method.

    e. Which Method to Use
Moreover, there are other methods and techniques of teaching. It is difficult to use any method without other methods entering into it. In any learning situation, a combination of methods is usually more effective than any one method alone.

Finally, evaluation must be integrated into the other aspects of the teaching-learning process.

It must be used in the motivation of the trainees; it must be used to assist in developing understanding during the training; and it must be related to employee application of the results of training.

This is distinctly the role of the supervisor.

www.ingramcontent.com/pod-product-compliance
Lightning Source LLC
Chambersburg PA
CBHW080322020526
44117CB00035B/2601